PRAISE FOR

"*The Painted Forest* is a surp
reader might be reminded of t
of Annie Dillard, the unrelenting gaze of Lia Purpura, or the masterful storytelling of Jo Ann Beard. Eastman is interested in interrogating the history and ethos of several specific places, including her own home state of Wisconsin, as well as elegantly demonstrating the ways in which landscapes shift and morph through generations and recall."

—Caryl Pagel, author of *Twice Told*

"*The Painted Forest* is a singular and visionary portrait of the Midwest, one that defies familiar caricatures of the region. Eastman puts rural towns and hamlets too often dismissed as 'nowhere' definitively on the map, and reveals that they are far more uncanny, complex, and bizarre than our wildest imaginings."

—Meghan O'Gieblyn, author of *Interior States*

"In this shimmering collection, Krista Eastman blends imagined scene with researched fact to bring us fresh visions of places we thought we knew. From examinations of home to 'laughter from nowhere,' from the Wisconsin Dells to Antarctica's McMurdo Station, from an itinerant painter's elliptical masterwork to gestation's feral undertow, Eastman casts a spell that renders us 'still captive to the mystery in distance, still loyal to the pledge found in story.'"

—Joni Tevis, author of *The World Is On Fire: Scrap, Treasure, and Songs of Apocalypse*

IN PLACE

Jeremy Jones, Series Editor
Elena Passarello, Series Editor

Far Flung: Improvisations on National Parks, Driving to Russia, Not Marrying a Ranger, the Language of Heartbreak, and Other Natural Disasters
Cassandra Kircher

Lowest White Boy
Greg Bottoms

On Homesickness: A Plea
Jesse Donaldson

KRISTA EASTMAN

The Painted Forest

West Virginia University Press
Morgantown 2019

First edition published 2019 by West Virginia University Press
Printed in the United States of America

ISBN
Paper 978-1-949199-19-2
Ebook 978-1-949199-20-8

Library of Congress Cataloging-in-Publication Data
Names: Eastman, Krista, author.
Title: The painted forest / Krista Eastman.
Description: First edition. | Morgantown : West Virginia University Press, 2019. | Series: In place
Identifiers: LCCN 2019013100| ISBN 9781949199192 (paperback) | ISBN 9781949199208 (eBook)
Subjects: LCSH: American essays–21st century. | Identity (Philosophical concept) | Place (Philosophy) | Wisconsin. | McMurdo Station (Antarctica)
Classification: LCC PS3605.A855 A6 2019 | DDC 814/.6–dc23
LC record available at https://lccn.loc.gov/2019013100

Book and cover design by Than Saffel / WVU Press
Cover and interior illustrations by Darumo Shop / DesignCuts

Essays in this collection previously appeared in the following publications: "Everybody Comes Round Here," *Sycamore Review*, issue 27, no. 2, Winter/Spring 2016; "Animals," *Kenyon Review Online*, Fall 2015; "The Painted Forest," *Sonora Review*, issue 67, Spring 2015; "Insider's Almanac," *The Georgia Review*, vol. LXVI, no. 2, Summer 2012; "Scrap Metal," *Hayden's Ferry Review*, issue 48, Spring/Summer 2011; "Middle West," *Cutbank*, issue 74, February 2011; "Wonder Spot," *The Massachusetts Review*, vol. 51, issue 4, Winter 2010; "Layers of Ice," *Witness*, vol. XXIII, 2010

For my parents

Contents

Scrap Metal (A Prologue)

This tubby steel machine, this 1978 Chevy Malibu station wagon, careens a large family forward, makes tinny the sound of our quarrels and questions while highway approaches and then unfurls behind, approaches and then unfurls. It is from this wagon that we view the sculptures, the scrap metal forms welded at weird angles onto themselves, forms that groan at ground in the way of all heavy equipment, but forms whose slanted reaches skyward warp and mock the object of industry. Here, out of nowhere, in the middle of nowhere, stands steel impracticality, love or whimsy or thought made big and embarrassing, material and metallic. They are painted. They are placed, purposively, along the road. We view and evade them by continuing at fifty-five miles per hour.

In this manner, we pass by over and over again, on our way to the capital to see the aunt, on our way to the capital for new school clothes. We start in a small Wisconsin town, pass up and over the Baraboo Bluffs, and then spill out onto a flat expanse of would-be prairie, where Highway 12 divides a U.S. Army ammunition plant, on the left, from a trailer park and junkyard, on the right. It's then that our eyes catch for a few full seconds, take in, for example, a flat, twenty-foot red heart stuck through with the scrap metal semblance of an arrow, before returning to the blur of roads, the blur of farmland once again. Our silence means, maybe, that we think this stretch of road strange, these oddities as resistant to what we, for our own comfort, might wish we could hang on them: learned vocabulary, confident appraisal, a more casual recognition.

For the length of my childhood, these sculptures climb higher. The blow torch of Tom Every, local scrap man, will eventually produce dozens of regal birds from old musical instruments, a 300-ton celestial launching pad called the Forevertron, and a steady gathering of the curious, pilgrims or passersby whose bodies register bafflement, joy, unexpected envy. Once, my quiet dad hazards a response. "I think they're kind of neat," he says, his eyes rolling sideways for spousal support. We're in a car on Highway 12 and the brave utterance cannot be taken back. From the window of our wagon, the coming road takes on a new and emerald sheen, the vast look of aftermath.

Insider's Almanac

On this sand farm in Wisconsin, first worn out and then abandoned by our bigger-and-better society, we try to rebuild, with shovel and axe, what we are losing elsewhere. It is here that we seek—and still find—our meat from God.

—Aldo Leopold, *A Sand County Almanac*

One way to share your home is to place it carefully, in a controlled way, onto someone else's map. Ceremoniously staring down at it for your guests also helps impress upon them that a new place unknown to them is right there being born. In an instance like this one, being the insider matters. *Are you from here? Yes*, you say, and then watch people step back further to study you, to visualize you in whatever watery picture they have of this little-known corner from which you come, to decide on what assumptions might offend, to feel suddenly stirred or just off balance on these, the warped boards of your family's century-long passing, this place that might have remained for them an irrelevant slope of soil.

This *from here*, my own admission of provenance, smells of vinegar and clamors to defend. Always it means the fixed-seeming mound of Wisconsin's Sauk County, a bit of earth that, despite my travels, I cannot get around, a place whose scar-like settlement, even on my most rational days, I cannot completely discount. This will be the first confession I make—my *from here* as your uneven ground, the strange ferocity with which any tiller looks over plots of imperfect earth.

—

Sauk County lies in southwestern Wisconsin, on the eastern edge of the Driftless. According to the poetry of geological nomenclature, this area lacks *drift*—is driftless. This is land left untouched by the most recent North American glaciations that ended here about 10,000 years ago. Here you will not find any of the features typically left in the wake of a glacier's melting back: no grit and gravel or foreign boulders, no perfectly rounded kettle lakes, no sweeping expanses where the ice once scraped the earth flat. Here instead are ancient hills, exposed bedrock more than 500 million years old, river valleys, long and handsome ridges, and the Baraboo River, which twists and turns as if slowly spinning in a skirt, boasting at a slow and languid pace of old age and apathy toward arrival. And, of course, where there used to be prairie and savanna, there is now mostly woods and farmland—green, luminescent, and industrial efforts at harvest reached by roads that must snake up, over, and around the gentle meander of this land.

The Driftless has been the site of settler colonialism and Euro-American farming for only a short while, about two hundred years, and yet that period has thoroughly rooted itself here, having hunkered down to birth this garden's original sin. My ancestors, that is, made room for themselves, rushing out to the plow on Ho-Chunk land stolen especially for them. In tending this soil, my family tended a myth, the one where a continent offered itself up to them a magnificent, fecund prize, where dispossession was but a small evil in service to a great God-given right. The brownish photographs in my mom's house show generations of this family, people in long white dresses or too-large suits, materializing ghostlike before trees and fields, or leaning on the kind of simple, whitewashed farmhouses that still punctuate turns on Sauk roads. These are sunburned-looking people with simple hair and shoes and expressions that give little away. The women chastely tote what we call "German birthing hips"—widely cast and generously enveloped in cushiony rump, the kind of female physiology believed conducive to birthing large farm boys. Eventually, machines start appearing and the photos lighten, turn into snapshots, wash out with sun. Posing casually next to these same machines are the men who look as hard as the steel they steered roughly over and into the land, altering the earth, plowing it under, extracting from it not just a livelihood but a culture, a way of life.

These were the families that knew all the other families living on all the same roads, who married one another or were suspicious of one another—the German Catholics, the Irish Catholics—but who rose every morning to work, whose presence became rooted, workaday, and conversational.

She was married to an Anderson, my Grandma Keller would begin while I listened in, there in the kitchen or out on the porch. *Okay, that must have been the younger brother of the Donny Anderson who was in my class*, Mom would reply. *Yes*, says Grandma slowly as she thinks, *see, there were five boys in that family and they lived on the old Kindschi farm, the one on the way to LaValle. But when they married, they built new towards Lime Ridge, that big red house—you know, at the elbow in the road, just down the road from the Wintermantels? Oh, sure!* Mom says and then pauses. *There's a lot of cancer in that family.*

Even I, not born until 1979, am still sometimes there and listening, still counting second cousins, still looking in.

—

In my imagination, a mythic male ancestor really could have trampled through wet morning grass to meet up with Aldo Leopold, a sometime neighbor but also the inchoate legend himself, the professor and early conservationist whose weekend shack in Sauk County was fodder for much of his environmental classic, *A Sand County Almanac*, published in 1949, after his death. Along adjoining property lines, the two men's feet would stand wrapped in a lovely stranglehold of native plants—natural phenomena for which I cannot imagine the names or shapes. Posed in stances sufficiently masculine and distanced, something suitable to 1946, they would share a silver thermos hot with coffee as they exercised their zest for rational thought, weather observations, talk of land. In this dream, farmer and professor sidle up alongside one another on soil marked Sauk County, casually straddle worlds, imbue the distant woodlots and slopes descending to marsh with the kind of note-taking that allows, quite organically, for nods and grunts and sidelong grins, the neighborly point of view.

What do we think might happen, my forebear would ask the professor in a hushed tone, *with the deer population this year?*

And yet here, already, is where the scene must end, interrupted as it is by the intervening smirk on the face of my composite character, a noncompliant man whom I recognize as my own (and whose shit-eating grin looks mysteriously like my maternal grandfather's). Here smiles at me a man who knows better than to fall for the truth as I would write it now, who will simply stride out of this role and head away from the sandy banks of the Wisconsin River and toward the Driftless, toward the portion of Sauk County where the farming is a bit better, where there are fields to mark with footprints, plow, dropped beads of sweat, and progress. I can tell even by the wobble of his gait that he is about to will an old prairie to produce, to wash away the topsoil of his back forty, to approach land in a way Aldo questions with learned and lyric precision.

Despite my best attempt to warn this ancestor of what the

future will bring, of how Leopold's celebrated "Land Ethic" essay will be written, he turns to walk back into his familiar obscurity, into the way farming has often been, the way he really was. And yet that wink, his quaint suggestion of our inside joke, also soothes me somehow. We two, you see, are both *from here*, an affiliation of sorts that counts as a fierce and unarticulated something. In fact, I am smiling lovingly at the sweat spot separating his now-distant shoulder blades when my loyalty gives me pause, makes me awkward.

Aldo Leopold, with his glasses and erect posture, the foreign good looks of a professor, has not gone anywhere, isn't missing a thing.

—

The girl version of myself, in her search to trace origins, couldn't get much further than the county line, and so she became first a fixture at the town's public library, then a traveler. And yet, local girl, avid reader, I never picked up *A Sand County Almanac*, the classic born just miles from my hometown, and I don't recall learning about it in school. My copy of Leopold's book, acquired in adulthood and in the spirit of research, smells of press and crispness, its pages not dog-eared nor tattered nor steeped in the oil found on fingertips. This almanac does not occupy my nightstand, has never been the binding I chose to brush up against in the dark, nor the words I intoned while on pilgrimage through the woods alone. But it has haunted me.

Reading *A Sand County Almanac*, I learned that Aldo Leopold made another kind of map of this place, providing the vocabulary for another way of looking at the world by transcribing the messages he found written on wind, dew, and pine with poetry and a pithy common sense. "There are some who can live without wild things, and some who cannot," he begins simply. "These essays are the delights and the dilemmas of one who cannot." And these words, like much of *A Sand County Almanac*, twist my thoughts. Arriving a little late to this book, this particular county, I must entertain my own share of new and uncomfortable questions, my own delights and dilemmas. Raised among open fields and cultivated hills, how will I be sure that I can or cannot live without these wild things, which I do not identify and cannot always see? I underline words such as *Silphium* and *bur oak* and wonder if these plants are still around. Have they been around all this time? Do they survive in the unharvested corners of farmland whose cultivated verdure most certainly plays me for a fool, prompting me to gaze as one gazes at the back of one's own hand, carelessly, with few questions?

A Sand County Almanac is part lyric manifesto, but it does much more than merely conjure up the natural beauty of Leopold's farm. Leopold also takes up the problem of perception, of how we perceive ourselves and the land we make our own—and the ethics of both of those things at once. In the chapter entitled "December," Leopold writes: "The wild things that live on my farm are reluctant to tell me, in so many words, how much of my township is included within their daily or nightly beat. I am curious about this, for it gives me the ratio between the size of their universe and the size of mine, and it conveniently begs the much more important question, who is the more thoroughly acquainted with the world in which he lives?"

Fueled by local affiliation, I approach this book with the same question, though mine conceals a different kind of curiosity. With sheepishness, I wonder about my mythic Leopold and myself, about the size of *our* two universes in this same Wisconsin county. I admit that asking the question this way risks placing the book in my hands at a perverse angle, exposing my interest as a brutish desire to defend, or to stake my own claim.

Leopold, measured and wise, continues: "Like people, my animals frequently disclose by their actions what they decline to divulge in words. It is difficult to predict when and how one of these disclosures will come to light."

Perhaps I should also decline to put into words the insularities of my own habitat. Like the many who've come before, perhaps I should brush off clear declarations in favor of physical work, express myself only with silent necessity—with eyes that know but hold back, with a stolid distaste for the process of explaining and, worse yet, of being explained. And yet disclosures have already been made, squatting with imperfection on my page and under my name. That made-up memory of the sweat spot I stood long enough to admire, has emboldened me somehow, causing me to speak almost by accident of another universe, another definition of *local*, the many ways you can wed yourself to land. Here I admit to animal behavior.

—

In the late 1940s, Leopold wrote, "There are two spiritual dangers in not owning a farm. One is the danger of supposing that breakfast comes from the grocery, and the other that heat comes from the furnace." By the 1980s, my close family did not farm and had not done so for twenty years. We lived in a small town of five thousand surrounded by dairy farms and, not so distantly, by even smaller towns surrounded by still more dairy farms. Once, we were "The Butter Capital of the World." That the farmers were struggling, we knew and supped on daily. That theirs was an honorable plight, we knew and believed. That our living had something to do with their struggle, we knew concretely, having for many years seen our dad and grandpa climb out of milk trucks after long days innumerable spent on milk route—often with a bag of the freshest cheese curds in hand, straight from the dairy and squeaky to chew. But, like most everyone else, we were townspeople who, on our way to a country bar for a Friday night fish fry, could only pass and point to the Family Farm—this one run by relatives, that one long ago sold.

On days off from my school, I accompanied my dad on his milk route, going along for the feeling of suspension high off the road, for the imagined sense of grown-up vocation. As Dad pulled into farm after farm, gathering up their daily production with a long suctioning hose and having taciturn interactions with the farmers, I delighted in eating the lunch packed for us by my mom as well as the variation in the farms' milk houses—some meticulously kept, some rough and rundown, each protecting a large steel container of milk, the air pungent with the bitter, full-body scent of milk fresh from the cow. I remember that the machines had silver and scientific-seeming dials, that the process of transferring milk from tank to truck was noisy. I remember a dog that chased excess milk around the drain and the series of sunburned farmers for whom I'd reprise my role as the milk hauler's daughter, pride lengthening my back. I remember climbing up and in again, gripping the bouncy black seat, admiring how Dad shifted gears, appreciating his important job and the truck's deep warble of industry.

Ours was a dairy connected to a large cooperative, but the farms were still small and family owned. The sound of the truck's diesel engine was the sound of us throwing our lot back in with them, out of solidarity perhaps, but out of economic opportunity too. And so, like many people *from here*, we found ourselves at a remove from the thing to which we also felt affiliated: the land that brought us here.

Today, our loyalty has grown deep on a sense of our own sweat and effort, but that loyalty has also become trickier to articulate, more difficult to evoke for others by way of authenticating detail. I can remember the milk truck perfectly, but then I fumble: suctioning tube, large steel container, a dog chasing milk down a drain, and that, over there, an old

Family Farm. Without a doubt, there exists the importance of pointing—often and proudly—to the distance. *Over there*, we say. *What we know.*

—

Claiming land for yourself is difficult to do without also exposing your depictions of ownership as false, unjustified, or incomplete, incapable of holding all the land's contradictions at once—too rooted, perhaps, in the vantage point afforded by your blindly digging fingers, the pull of your own stomach. And yet there are some practical reasons for making the attempt. For example, others will define what you will not. They will draw you in the kind of broad strokes that make the little lie of nostalgia glorious to behold. Here the small grocery, there a man they call salt of the earth, here the crumbling red barn, there the Holsteins standing against a blue sky, placed like a bygone portrait on the spine of that ridge. Of course, holding the desperate power of the one who can define, she who is *from here* and so appoints herself, doesn't preclude the possibility of hypocritical reversals, when suddenly the insider can also invent any number of convenient lies, tall tales extolling seemingly regional virtues: Wheels of cheese large as Buicks roll into town each Saturday! The air? It smells fresh and sweet and is laden with the preponderance of honesty dewing all this small-town sweat. *From here*, she will say, an ax hitting the block of her province each time.

Hands gritty with this problem of depiction, with the controversy of claiming a place for one's own, I begin to touch other questions. Defining this Nowhere—this Elsewhere, Wisconsin—may require language that allows for contradiction, language that exposes the frequent error of my remarks. It may require tempering my guttural assertions with occasions of polite and reasoned awareness, learned acknowledgments of larger points of view. And yet these diplomatic allowances cannot sweep away that something still there, that question I might never get around: who will count as being acquainted with the world in which he lives?

Probing the quality of one's most basic connections—to hills, to family, to centuries of their interweaving—risks an unraveling, is difficult to do. Standing with your feet still wrapped in the sheen of nonnative crops, affiliation with one's land can seem knee deep, a thing unto itself, so apparent it's only disclosed from time to time in subtle nods to the neighbor met on the road: He who also owns and works and cultivates, he who also makes claims on slopes not so far from here. He who knows that if connection to land were judged in knowing nods to his neighbor, he'd emerge from the scrutiny of all measurements an undisputed Earth King, widely known and well liked, custodian of common cause.

—

I couldn't call this a quest, couldn't shape this as an attempt to answer a question—about affiliation, about localness, about being *from here*—without also leaning into my own sizeable gaps in knowledge of the land. And so I called on a trained botanist, a prairie expert, and we walked into the Curtis Prairie, a restored tall grass prairie of the University of Wisconsin's arboretum. He moved forward with eyes and nose cast toward the ground, placed the palm of his hand around the back of some wisp standing in a vast pointillism of green, bent the sprig toward me, identified it: common name and scientific name, the surprising members of its family. This arboretum, like many of Wisconsin's conservation legacies, exists because of the vision of Aldo Leopold and his university colleagues who, in 1934, began to transform this fallow farmland into the landscapes that were abundant before widespread agriculture. The arboretum—now cut in two by a major highway and enveloped by the capital city of Madison—includes some of the country's oldest and most diverse ecological restorations.

This botanist tended to watch my perfunctory plant examinations, the way I didn't seem to be retaining all of this, with one part despair and one part hope, then he'd walk on before reaching for another plant and turning back to wait for me to draw closer, his eyes peering through tips of grass again. To him this broad swath of prairie, otherwise blurring into collective elegance, contained hundreds of hidden individuals, plants with names, needs, and distinct roles in the life of the prairie. I scratched down the names of plants encountered. Under grasses I wrote: Indian grass, big blue stem. Under forbs: purple coneflower (*Echinacea*), compass plant (*Silphium*), bush prairie clover, goldenrod, rattlesnake master, blazing star, indigo, and sumac. This, I felt, was the deep capture of detail.

I wrote down their names because I knew that I would not otherwise remember them, but I also focused on walking elsewhere, on the hills of Sauk County, where I envisioned prairie or savanna, open land punctuated only by what I now knew to be bur oak, that occasional curmudgeon, a tree with bark so thick it will not and cannot burn. I walked where I could see more precisely the fires that would have licked these hills clean, burning off trees and shrubs, making room for the lush intricacy of living prairie, for the tangled thicket that would have curled into delicate explosions of nerve and grace, giving cover, providing a secret place. In my mind I stretched one stratum up and over the other, communed for a moment with the life smothered by my provenance, felt a distant tragedy. But then, growing irritable with the effort of my own hapless imagining, I began to pick burs off my long cotton skirt with an almost hysterical sense of their nuisance. I scowled at them, stuck as they were on all sides and at all heights, everything in that moment seeming caught up in the simple burden of my having passed by, here where everything and nothing got left to the breeze.

From the Curtis Prairie, we passed through the Leopold Pines, through the dank and unlit tunnel under the beltline highway, through the Old Field, along the Grady Oak Savanna, down into the Greene Prairie where the foliage crested at my knees. The narrow boardwalk, raised just inches above the wet soil, extended along a crowded path through this low grass prairie. Forty acres of an immeasurable-seeming thickness surrounded us. Thin grass leaves wound themselves up, around, and into the weblike rondure of plants posing in grass-cradling arabesques. It was possible to gaze down on their intricacy, to look right down into the realization that the rest of this green expanse, hazing in the distance, contained the same density held here by my immediate gaze.

"This is a wet prairie," my botanist explained, his eyes distracted, his feet pacing every inch of the boardwalk as he twisted about, attempting to register each plant at once: prairie cordgrass (*Spartina pectinata*), leadplant (*Amorpha canescens*), nodding lady's tresses (*Spiranthes cernua*) . . .

The lowland, infused that day by mottled sun, had the dim luster of an everyday spectacular, as if to emphasize that this beauty existed, just as it was, even on the most ordinary of days, even when all people busy themselves far away from here, under dull cloud covers, on Tuesdays. The prairie's almost clandestine existence, situated quite a way beyond the underground tunnel, became for me the cause of some anguish. How did the simple act of seeing the prairie become a trip, a journey to accidental secrecy, requiring a map and concerted movement under a highway and across some fields? My fellow traveler told me that this area, all forty acres of it that remain, was hand planted in the 1940s and '50s by a mycologist named Henry Greene, who restored his prairie alone. Greene was supposed to have been a character, and my guide marveled at the idea of one person's hands having graced every plant here.

I, who can often live without wild things, could not live without them in that moment. *The Greene Prairie*, I said to myself, my own breath becoming a self-conscious thing. *The . . . Greene . . . Prairie*. I imagined one man bent low over this field, spending long hours alone next to some train tracks, on the southernmost edge of the arboretum, making a model of what once was, placing seeds in the earth in silent protest of everything at once: widespread tillage, notions of the bigger and the better, the singsong lilt of the university's cocktail chatter, or the unwitting heartbeats of crowds defined by their not knowing that any of this was even here. Over and over, Henry Greene would have placed seeds for which he had proximate hopes, but from time to time he would also have entertained visions of a larger scale, pushing his inchoate plans into the earth, just for the moment storing them there.

The botanist pointed out a thick beige line wrapping around two edges of the prairie. This sweeping front is the look and livelihood of reed canary grass, an invasive that moves into and colonizes areas disturbed by development, pushing everything else out. Like some nefarious superhero, canary grass will not burn and cannot otherwise be stopped. It encroaches on the Greene Prairie every year, having already swallowed up ten of the original sixty acres. No amount of research has deduced a way of pushing it back.

Behind the reed canary grass, up on a small wooded ridge, stood the backside of new houses, a development rising beyond the boundary between private property and arboretum. My eye moved from the new siding of these boxy homes to their gray shingles to the lowlands in the foreground and the canary grass advancing, its powerful homogeneity never failing to fall to the ground and give birth to replications. Then I scanned all the way back to Henry Greene's prairie and the diversity still entangling itself at my feet, an example of what-had-been now caught in a dramatization of how the prairie disappeared. "And this," said the botanist, gesturing toward the advance of the canary grass, "is analogous to what happened with agriculture."

Standing on the boardwalk, looking at that beige line, I contemplated refusing to leave. *Stop*, I could have screamed there, over and over again, until someone or something finally took notice. But this was a hidden place, gotten to through a highway tunnel long, dark, and damp. The heartbeats of people, those defined by their not knowing, would merely power their cars past my protest, on the highway, en route to work or the store, never hearing my voice, and I would be there not even knowing what to say if once I gained their attention.

I turned to leave the prairie behind and wallow in a melancholy that reminded me yelling is but one method. The language on my tongue slipped into the formulas of elegy and lament, wound into a dirge tilting toward the lovely and the lovelorn before coming out onto a final silencing *shhhh*. Though nothing had been halted, I was momentarily released. In gloomy quiet I slid away, wondering what it was my feet would touch in the highway tunnel and in the life on the other side of that darkness.

Meanwhile, on days with dull cloud cover, the ghost of Henry Greene works from dawn to dusk, pulls out reed canary grass one stalk at a time, mocks my cocktail chatter, searches for an idea he thinks he buried once. *It must be here*, the prairie says to him over and over again. *It must be here*, Greene repeats, a knee-deep invocation.

—

You've got to drive to see what's on the other side of the Greene Prairie. A city bus passing by this widely cast entrance—brick pillars and a sign suggesting expanse, wealth, and managed nature—would have few requests to stop here. The cloistering spirit of suburbia, with its deep allegiance to the car, has constructed these streets' widely arcing curves, has sculpted the logic of these curbs and the thick lawns spilling down to them.

I pulled into the entrance with a nervous feeling of infiltration. Drawing force from the book *PrairyErth (A Deep Map)*, in which William Least Heat-Moon spends twelve hours observing a small Kansan town from behind the curtains of his van, I planned to park my car and look inconspicuous all afternoon. I would pull out a notebook, look for signs of inhabitants and insider acts of affiliation, and then try to articulate what I supposed to be the way of life here. Failing that, I'd gain at least a different view of the Greene Prairie.

But soon I got lost and carsick on the turns of the development. On the left, on the right, I passed what appeared to be five- and six-bedroom homes squatting on the sculpted pedestals of grassy lots, but I saw no one stirring. I directed myself toward what I assumed would be the prairie, but always I ended up twisting out onto more curving roads with more homes. I began to feel seized by panic, realizing that this was not a neighborhood for casual stopping, for motorists without driveway destinations. Eventually I saw some people, or rather some signs of them: cargo vans advertising plumbing, electrical work, painting, and lawn care. I considered these teams of people called in for upkeep, and I heard the words of Aldo Leopold: "The whole world is so greedy for more bathtubs that it has lost the stability necessary to build them, or even to turn off the tap. Nothing could be more salutary at this stage than a little healthy contempt for a plethora of material blessings."

In the eerie silence of this abandoned opulence, I wondered at how easy it can be to take resources for one's own. Haunted by Greene Prairie, I wondered what "a little healthy contempt" would look like, how it would work, how much of it would be allowed, and who would have the human faces toward which, after knocking on these doors, I'd have to politely extend my disgust.

I was driving on, making turns that by this time had lost all meaning and which had long since scattered my feeling for the Greene Prairie's location, when finally I came upon them: They were blond and wiry. They moved with sharp uptakes of energy as seven- or eight-year-old legs propelled their bodies off concrete, into sky. Defying the constraints suggested for them by their driveway and habituated to the neighborhood's quiet, one boy, all hands and thighs and ankles, shimmied up the black pole of his basketball hoop while the other watched. As I came closer, they both turned to stare at me with the likeness of brothers not too far apart in age, their expressions similarly curious and unimpressed. I kept driving forward but also felt free to turn my head and stare right back, the boys' twin suspicion rising to meet me, protecting them, in a moment of instinct, against a stranger's interest.

Turning onto a street named Leopold Way, moving as the streets there moved me, I left the exchange of stares behind, the boys having long ago gained their ground. They, I realized, will never need to travel to see what's on the other side of the Greene Prairie, not as prospectors with a notion to build and not as trespassers ready with a critique. Because these boys were born of this seeded grass, their home will not seem new to them but as old and natural as the dawn of their own breathing. And the day might even come when they, too, will decide to define their provenance and thus explain and extol the virtues of all this—their patch of grass, their sense of sidewalk.

Indeed, in response to the insinuations of a lowly essayist, she who grew emboldened by her one-time visit to their next-door prairie, they might lean against that basketball pole of their youth, with grown-man feet pressing dominion down onto the driveway of their mother's home, and claim insider knowledge, stating that a new place, hitherto unknown or misunderstood, is about to be added to my map. They might tell me what I don't know—point to insider facts, list the ways this place provided. *We're from here*, they would say, assuring me that, indeed, their affiliations do stand for something.

But there exist always, I think, other possibilities. When the eldest, the master of pole climbing, turns out to be the better student (diligent and ambitious), he might travel east to college, settle into a dorm room, look through his paned window, and see that in his first move away from home he has come upon an ancient New England town, the oldest place he's ever known. In response to his new East Coast friends, they who like to tease him at parties, he will boast of Wisconsin's cheese and microbrews, pander to the crowd by conjuring up the regional quirkiness of the state's love for polka, or the over-the-top friendliness of the people, or the beauty of the hills he'll call "undulating" because the word itself gathers up all the loose strings of his comedy. He might claim other connections too, as they become fashionable or useful, as he learns about leaving and going back and leaving again, as he comes to name and adapt to his universe of one. *From here*, he'll then say, with one part nostalgia, one part absence, putting what he needs on his back, readying his connections for the road, leaving in search of home.

—

Back in my bedroom, as a child, I woke to a refrain:

No, she was the oldest. Marilyn was the middle, Mom says.

—Oh, yes, that's right. It was Barbara, Marilyn, and then Judy.

And she's the one who moved out west somewhere. —Colorado, wasn't it? —Yes, that's right. Well, the farm came up at auction and Ruby said it was bought by Steve Schonfeld. It's the one just down the road from the old Lutheran church . . . and so the girls were all back in town last week, and, boy, were they upset about selling it. —Oh, really? —Well, I think it was Marilyn who went out to eat at Longley's the day after. She stops to talk to me and she tells me all three of them cried at the auction, at the sale of the farm. —Really? My mom says again, this time her question's intonation dropping in sympathy. *Well, I bet they did,* she continues. *That was their home for a long time, but now, you know, they all live so far. It just wouldn't make much sense for them to keep it. —No, I guess it wouldn't,* Grandma says. *And you know the Schonfeld that bought it, he's gonna work it. —And that's just it,* Mom concludes. Even from my bedroom I know them to be exchanging glances marked by pragmatism and wistfulness as they take simultaneous sips of coffee.

When I try to imagine and then catalog the ways my mom misses her own mother, I always think first of this: the manner of their talking and its importance, too, the conversational upkeep required for seeing these hills, each and every one of them, as a hill apart—patches of earth marked by the homes of different families, and each of those families made of the oldest, the youngest, the one having spent some time in jail. Their conversations spanned land owned and land lost, stories of grief and envy, stories of weariness and work, the fact of the children moving away, and the fact of the children coming back again. Talking to one another, they made a detailed map of this particular county, reciting lineages, naming newcomers, and looking on these hills with a kind sense of story, a keen eye for progeny.

Spiranthes cernua, Grandma says matter-of-factly, with great calm.

Amorpha canescens, Mom says, nodding.

—

Who is the more thoroughly acquainted with the world in which he lives? One answer, skeptical, and in part: whosoever can produce the most detail.

—

Another way to share your home is to leave it with due care, pushing off from your provenance, whether on foot or on thought. To pack a bag with some food, blankets, and a compass, use the bathroom one last time. To announce what everyone gathered long ago, that your affiliations, though deeply felt, are like the land itself: cultivated, contested, grown from contradiction and tilled by circumstance, by the muscle of the people you knew, by the beating hearts of those who sought and then succeeded in feeding you. Once you've made this final admission, you can release the weary guests who might remain by leading them across the porch, past the garden, back around the fixed-seeming mound of Sauk County. You can continue to walk them well past the county line, past

Leopold's shack, past any number of county lines while braving highway tunnels and crossing rivers, while considering the sweat that collects on every shoulder blade.

With what, my mythic Leopold might ask, a fire in his eye, *must we first become acquainted?*

Don't know yet, the forebear grunts to him sidelong, placing a boot down on the blade of a steel shovel, digging for the two of them other ways to belong and another place to know, a tunnel traveling into the center of this earth.

Wonder Spot

The Dells of the Wisconsin River (1856): *For Recreation Resort to the Dells! Where depressed spirits can be alleviated, gloom and melancholy soon be dispelled and the mind become Greatly invigorated. Leroy Gates has purchased a pleasure Boat for the purpose of penetrating the numerous occult caves of the Dells.*

Evidence of human attempts at luring are here in all these excavated lots and parcels, these sums of money once borrowed from the bank, this old resort cabin now sheltering earwigs and mice, the Eastern European college students who wake to interim American lives, to jobs as fudge confectioners or laser tag cashiers. This small Wisconsin settlement, the kind of town that might have centered itself around the Catholic Church, the family farm, the local tavern, instead hunkers down on the banks of the Wisconsin River, surveys the sandstone scenery banking upriver and down, and takes its communion by peering down at the promise that never stops eddying in froth and darkness here. It was from this spot, or these "Dells," that local river pilot Leroy Gates first made the bid in 1856 to beckon the tourists forth. An offer of "Great invigoration"—later coupled with stereoscopic photos of the place—would generate the eager eye and middle-class pocketbook of the new nineteenth-century tourist: the Chicagoan, the Milwaukeean, the men working the desks of Saint Paul. From the start, there were tourists and there were locals; currency, that is, to be removed from your pocket and placed into mine.

In 1960, John Steinbeck became one of the many tourists to pass by here in answer to Gates's call. Born of a short stay occurring more than fifty years ago, his written observations are oddly complete. He mused over a seashell collection, one he was surprised to find in a place "which hasn't known a sea since pre-Cambrian times." He didn't fail to note "the merchants of the cheap and mediocre and tawdry," but he also approached the river with awe, speculating that its unusual rock formations might contain "the engraved record of time when the world was much younger and much different." When all present-day jet skis cease to advertise their individualism, having sputtered back to port for the night, the river and its formations do still suggest and invite a keeping and recording of time. These sandstone cliffs have the sedimentary look of history after history rolled out, a delicate sequencing, a careful brushing down. Up close, there is a beauty and endurance peculiar to this place—to this soft orange bedrock smelling strangely of five hundred million years gone by, and to the dank and secret quality of the river's caves, canyons, and gulches. But again, up close, a similar level of scrutiny reveals other sorts of records being kept here, ledgers on profits and ensnarement, lists engraved on the lips of good witnesses, locals who will not forget.

Still alive are the names of the many boats that have traveled this river in remunerated quests for scenery, "Indian" culture, and the fresh air of the Wisconsin wild: the steamboats *Modacowanda*, *Dell Queen*, and *Winnebago*; the all-steel twin screws *Red Cloud* and *Marquette*, *Joliet* and *Yellow Thunder*; and now—given the current appetite for jet boat thrill rides—the nameless blurs performing splashy "power stops" before towering cliffs of sandstone. *Fast,* this is the newest promise made here on a river whose man-made dams have entirely reined in its once pregnant rise to rapids. And yet the river, and its role as watery platform for escape, is no longer even the half of it, just as the jet boat's offer to transport you quickly is now far from the only one of its kind. One hundred fifty years of fabricated attraction will give way to some of the most varied offers ever made here on Earth: a deer park with large signage that has advertised the opportunity to

FEED AND PET THE DEER!

since local time immemorial; restaurants, hotels, mini-golf courses, water parks, and bars themed to suggest you are (all at once) in the Caribbean, encountering Native American traditions, living like Paul Bunyan, on an African safari; and generously numerated offers like this one: "37 steep and slippery slides, 6 hair-raising roller coasters and 8 curve-hugging go-kart tracks, all sitting on 156 acres of adventure." These days, it is not enough for a store to simply stand ready to be entered, offering only itself or its contents. Something must also be promised in big bold letters, lest the store go unnoticed by eyes just then taking in thirty other offers to exchange. Here, everyone understands perfectly when you emblazon

YOU NEED IT? WE GOT IT!

on a panel stretching the entire length of your store's exterior wall. The skies just behind this same panel fill with roller coasters that pile on one truss at a time, cranking out mechanical routes to the heavens.

And yet as eyewitness I might be guilty of something here. I've begun with a bit of natural beauty, given it the sheen of gold, and then finished with a physical cobbling on, a smorgasbord of plastic thrills grown large enough to obscure the hearts of people and noisy enough to silence entirely what could be the sound of a river if, in fact, the sound of the river was the descriptive detail that got chosen. When faced with so many neon grabs for the pot, it is tempting to paint only with the wide strokes of Americana, or to lay the ground work for an easy allegation of greed and consumerism all around. It is easy, again almost natural, to classify tourists as materialist drones consuming the world in increments and pieces, just as it is also easy to define the local population by their open pockets. Harder, though, is to put one's finger on the Everyplace pieced together by these transactions. "Escape," the bumper sticker used to read, "to Wisconsin." To this town come people who wander in awkward states of not knowing and not known, who surrender much and surrender often in their search for escape. Promises flicker and twist at a dizzying pace. Eddying, after all, is when water doubles back, turning out a small whirl.

—

The Wonder Spot (1952–2006): *No one stands erectly, sees correctly or walks a straight line as things that appear to be quite normal are just the opposite. You'll be mystified at what you experience in this small corner of the world where the laws of nature have gone awry. Would you believe that your sense of balance and perspective have deserted you? Water flows uphill, pendulums hang crookedly, and chairs balance on only two legs. The Wonder Spot defies the law of gravity as natural forces tilt you up to unexplainable angles. Discovered in 1948, the Wonder Spot has baffled its visitors for over 40 years. You have to see it to believe it!*

The Captain bounces on wiry muscle and loose joints, shoots the river his grin.

"This. Place. Is. Funny." He stands in ritual at the helm of his small tour boat, his hand fidgeting on the innermost circle of its wooden wheel. It appears he's seen something on shore and this something has set him to smiling. Leaning away from the controls, he pours himself another Styrofoam cup full of coffee and adjusts the black locks he keeps pushed up into a cap. "What?" I ask, "What is it?"

"This place is fun-ny!" the Captain says again, this time in a dark tavern downtown where a bachelorette party, recently alighted from its rental bus, plays "Suck for a Buck," offering men the opportunity to suck Lifesavers off the T-shirted breasts of the intoxicated bride-to-be.

This Captain could tally up more than five decades of living here, more than enough time to observe purchased discovery playing out in vacation-long increments, or to see each Memorial Day bring in a new crew of workers, any of whom might eventually disappear into the relief of Labor Day, their pockets heavy with cash and anonymous leave-taking. A middle-aged man who has supped again and again from the fountain of youth, the Captain's bearing nonetheless shows a stalwart accumulation of years. His "Welcome aboard" and "Sit back and relax" and "Thank you, come visit us again" are easy and unforced. And yet, in private, he speaks in language measured by years of analysis and theory. His is the speculative language of the researcher who has undertaken a lifelong study, who, upriver and down, navigates the same five miles of river, over and over again asking why.

When visiting the Captain at work, I stand at his boat's entrance, hands clasped behind my back, feet cast slightly apart, smiling and greeting each of his customers as they board. I also spring off the boat as it's docking, grabbing its lines and twisting it into half hitches on the cleat, smiling once again. "Have a good night," I can't help but say to his passengers, an old, practiced sincerity automating all over again. Compared to the Captain, I have put in only a few years of study here. Ushered into the adult world at least partially by the experience of working in this town, emerging from it with what may be the requisite amount of skepticism, I worked summers here from ages fourteen to twenty-two, spending the last four of those years as a tour guide on the river, at the heart of the oldest industry, either holding a microphone to my flapping mouth, or floating pleasantly about the small all-steel vessel as I asked my brood of eighty if they had any questions.

"How deep's the river?"

Generally speaking most of the river we're traveling on today is about thirty to forty feet deep, but we do travel over a section that is about eighty feet deep. I'll point that out to you as we come to it.

"Why's the water so brown?"

Because of a natural substance called tannin or tannic acid, which is found in the tamarack and hemlock trees that grow north of here, and which naturally makes its way into the water. Actually, a lot of ponds and lakes in northern Wisconsin are also similarly dark in color.

"Miss, what did you say you're majoring in?"

English and French.

"What are you going to do with *that*? Teach?"

Is it after two years of this work or two days that all tourists start to seem the same? Come morning, passengers board, come evening, they disembark. The sun will then rise on the group of them, in line with tickets, waiting again the next day. After a while, there is no question you've never been asked, few kids you haven't seen smacked. There are hardly any religions to which you haven't been converted, no accent you can't place. Even tourists who grow self-conscious and clever, who watch you in just such a way, who want you to know they realize full well that this, their change of scenery, is your everyday grind, who are capable of remarks that mock this place, this tour, this tourism, even these people are merely an average day to you. Such repetition should make it difficult to keep watching. And yet after purveying your daily myth, after sitting down in final silence, smile turned off, the boat heading back to port, it's good to be wary, to wonder at these passengers who doze and cuddle, who relax all of a sudden, who have hastily rummaged through your offer of escape until at last—experiencing something, experiencing nothing—a silence falls and not a single desire can be heard over the bellow of the boat's Chevy engines.

In sociologist Dean MacCannell's classic *The Tourist: A New Theory of the Leisure Class*, he writes, "Just as the great lighted signs at Las Vegas can be converted into sights, it is possible to transform the tourists themselves into attractions." The tourists, yes, but everything else too, every single wayside promise. When the Captain says to me yet again, "This place is funny," I know the moment well, but I know it by the impulse he has helped work into my bones, the way the refrain keeps me on course. The sentence may fall in mystery from the Captain's lips, but what he means is that there's never a bad time to lay claim to your wonder, to take a long look around, to wryly catalog how the laws of nature can astound.

—

Xanadu (1980–1990): *The original Xanadu was a palace seen in a poet's dream. . . . A house built of insulation. A house which is inexpensive and energy efficient: solar heated and furnished with appliances and conveniences which are guaranteed to influence home design. The basis of Xanadu's construction is the spraying of polyurethane foam insulation on the inside of large hemispheric balloons. After the foam cures, the balloons are removed, leaving a very strong dome structure resistant to the elements. Tour at your leisure 12 newly decorated contiguous domes featuring: Balloon Form Construction, Climate Room & Spa, Home Computer, Solar Collector, Champagne Glass Bed, Children's "Swiss Cheese" Room, Wind Generator Room, Habitat Room, Super Spa, and Geodesic Room. Xanadu is a practical and plausible application of futuristic products of today.*

I imagine Chuck Anderson, Master Teacher, to have been here once or twice when still a little boy, a child meandering down river roads that in his day were lined with little more than a humble series of small cabin resorts. That's purely conjecture and yet, being a Chicagoan, what a local might call a FIB (fucking Illinois bastard), it's quite likely that the Master Teacher was a tourist in the Dells before buying real estate here. From 1992 until his death in 2008, Master Teacher built here a spiritual community formally known as the New Christian Church of Full Endeavor. It would grow to include dormitories, a Miracles Healing Center, the Endeavor Academy, several businesses, and at least one satellite campus abroad. And while the New Age persuasion of those entering the academy might suggest that physical location is beside the fact, I couldn't help but notice that the academy's location wasn't beside the point, not quite. Instead, it was beside the Dells of the Wisconsin River, beside promise upon promise already whirling for well over a century, promises already gathering car-bound crowds come to be altered on site.

During Master Teacher's lifetime, the Endeavor Academy was known to many locals as simply "The Cult," a designation shared by some former members as well as the cult expert Rick Ross, who told CBS News in 1999 that "it appears to be a destructive cult." Outside its oldest and largest restaurant, one of several sources of community income, sat the occasional car or two, "For Sale" signs in the windows marking someone's decision to enter what Master Teacher called the "mind training." In those early years, it was difficult for locals to know or understand what was happening inside. The new community members' reluctance to socialize with outsiders plus the town's natural proclivity for gossip and suspicion together ensured that the academy remained shrouded in almost titillating mystery. The Captain had a friend who used to be one of the academy's food suppliers. "Trust me," the Captain said to me one day, mouth full of mirth, "he could tell you stories."

For most, a trip to the restaurant provided the easiest window in. A converted cheese factory with decor eerily suggestive of, say, a future-obsessed 1953, the restaurant also featured an old, immaculate soda fountain, a glass case operating as leisurely carousel of large, frosted desserts, and a half dozen lean and attractive waitstaff, people whose accents often revealed other native tongues and whose bowties or flowery skirts fused odd bits of disparate kitsch—something like the favorite sweater of rural Austria meeting the bobby socks of the all-American, silver-streaked diner. The atmosphere strove for throwback but also remained strangely monochromatic, pleasantly flat, as if it were a powder someone had been charged with blowing in through the vents. On any one visit, those same lean and attractive waitstaff would wander to and fro tables, untouched by all stress or urgency, joyfully delivering high-fat and high-sugar vegetarian foods, the consumption of which tended to override all autonomy, leaving you inert, heavy, vulnerable. *What just happened?* I'd take to wondering yet again as I waddled out the double doors full and curious, stopping only to drop more of my suspicion onto the giant stocks of flowers lining the entrance's pathway. It was here, at this restaurant, that I also saw the Master Teacher in person for the first and only time. An old man with falsely black hair, he walked slowly into the restaurant with a smile tucked into the elastic folds of his lips. The sight of him caused the staff to illuminate on the spot, elation seeming to push their bodies up on the tips of their toes, an eagerness to be noticed by him raising their shoulders.

On another visit many years later, I picked up a free Master Teacher DVD entitled *The Production of the Story of a Course in Miracles* on display near the register. I took it home and watched breathlessly as the Master Teacher shuffles onto camera, removing his jacket. He nods, says, "Hello. Hello," his cartoonish eyebrows shaped like vise grips coming together and pushing apart again, his shoulders bobbing as if to music. "Are you okay?" he asks almost inaudibly, breaking again and again into an intense smile, an almost joyous smirk, that lasts uncomfortably long. Through much of the DVD, he leans towards the camera, a forearm on his knee, with tiny dark eyes staring so relentlessly at the camera that his blinking feels monumental, his lids opening and closing on some other world. Devoted to my wonder, I transcribed, connecting his words, assembling his sentences.

> This is a very special day because in the mind training, you've decided to take the spirit of energy of love and multiply it in the idea, okay, of, in the idea of being, well, here in this cycle, aren't you? . . .

> Now, obviously the problem that you have is when you examined it in your frame, I become what you think is an eighty-year-old body with all sorts of memory. I don't do that. I don't know how to do that. I've taken a frame of reference of the joy I'm feeling about myself and letting it represent the small location in which I find myself by not resisting the idea and accumulating something else within my mind. What am I actually doing in the miracle? Shortening time. . . .
>
> Reminding you that you can shorten the interval of time in which you're representing yourself with a whole universe out there, okay, 14,000 million years it's been out there, and you've been here for a fraction of a second, and what you do is, rather than let it accumulate in you, you take a hold of it and you hang onto it and have another instant of death within your own association. . . .
>
> It's going to make you very happy.

At certain intervals, text scrolls vertically on the screen, disappearing as Master Teacher's voice reads it. Other times music is played, a welcome reprieve from the work of figuring out how to shorten time. And Master Teacher often sings along. When "Unchained Melody" begins playing, Master Teacher's wrinkled eyes turn to pour out their love, and he gazes down at the camera as if looking down into the tear-streaked face of God himself. "You're the one I've been looking for," Master Teacher says. There is a pause. "A conversion technique of the energy of reflected light can bring you an image as suddenly right now as it did a thousand years ago. . . . A thousand years from now. I'm going to show you." There is a pause. And then—right then—the Righteous Brothers chime in on perfect cue, a high-pitched "I ne-eeed your love," and Chuck Anderson, Master Teacher, smiles.

Twice this man will focus his small and earnest eyes on my own, lean into and across the screen's plane, violate our otherwise easy separation, and say to me with a touch of amusement, "I'm the Master Teacher. I don't get old, I can't get sick, and I don't die!" After I hear it the second time, I stop the DVD and take off for elsewhere, for the kitchen, where I plunge fingers into dishwater, eager just then for my hands to do earthly work. Chuck Anderson, as it's beginning to turn out, promises what could be a startling occurrence, a miracle. The Master Teacher, having escaped a universe tyrannized by the time dimension, offers up the mind vacation, eddying without end.

—

Stand Rock Indian Ceremonial (1929–1997): *Greetings friend! And an invitation from the Native Americans of Wisconsin Dells to join in our celebration of Life . . . and Love of Country, through the art of ancient tribal dances. Performed nightly under the stars in a beautiful, natural rock ampitheatre* [sic]. *An educational treat for the entire family!*

We became fluent in nonsense. *Our next point of interest will soon be sliding into view on your right. You're looking for a formation that resembles a buttery stack of pancakes.* Studded with what we call "points of interest," the boat tour was often like this, like it had almost always been. Points of interest are rock formations sculpted by *wind, water, and frost erosion*, and imagined into a variety of shapes: Chimney Rock, the Baby Seal, the Naked Lady, the Navy Yards, Hawk's Beak, Fat Man's Misery, Demon's Anvil. In fact, few outcroppings of rock or fern-lined ravines went unnamed here, where the tour boats have for years passed all day long, from April to October, a guide directing peoples' gazes to the same views again and again. Our words placed stories and likenesses onto silent bits of rock and root (Giant's Shield! Sunset Cliffs! Steamboat Rock!), making tidy increments of this sliver of universe. We knew that this particular iteration of *escape*—the suggestion of new air, new experience, the bittersweet loveliness of one's own wake—would be recognizable to many. That it would stand mapped and ready for pre-prescribed discovery, its own collective taking.

As the captain swings the boat around, two towering cliffs on either side of the river will soon be sliding into view on the starboard side of the vessel. I'd been barely aware of speaking, or facing my passengers, or using my left arm to point straight out at the cliffs, or of the eyes that clambered along the angle of that same arm, straining to see what it was I told them to. *Called the Lower Jaws of the Upper Dells, or sometimes the Gateway to the Upper Dells, these cliffs mark the official start of our tour here today.* I did notice, however, that a couple in their late thirties sitting just before me, cozying up to the helm, smiled as they leaned forward and into my tour. Watching them now and again, my words ran along unchecked and I thought about different things altogether. *Off to the right side of the bank is High Rock, rising about sixty feet out of the water. And, if you scan over to the left, that's—uh—.* What was the name of that one? I'd identified it a thousand times before, most recently, in fact, two hours previously.

"Romance Cliff!" the couple in front whispered to me simultaneously, leaning toward me in swooping rescue. The man, his manner conspiratorial, mouthed the words to me again, earnestness in the round *O* of his eyes: "Ro-mance. Cliff." Later this couple would tell me they'd taken this tour dozens of times, that they loved it here, that they came back each year for their anniversary. But in that moment my stuttering, my grappling for the right name, stretched longer still, the boat's passengers all waiting now for my sentence to finish unfurling itself. I stood silent, microphone in hand.

This is Romance Cliff, and it stands about seventy-five feet out of the water, I finished, feeling somehow chastened by this nice couple, now calm and nodding. *Generally speaking the waters we'll be traveling over today are about thirty to forty feet deep. We will, however, pass over some spots in excess of eighty feet deep, and I'll be sure to point those out to you as we come to them.* Again, I was back on track and talking but still I turned to something else. I wondered at my part in excavating this place's promises, bringing them to life in language, asking of everyone all day every day, *Do you see it? Do you see Beauty A, B, and C?* [Pause.] *Beauty D approaches.*

Once, worn out and close to done with my job for the season, I stumbled into an accidental experiment in the unscripted. I said to a tourist, "The Devil took over the Dells in 1962," and then immediately regretted it. Unlike the many canned responses I'd honed over several seasons of guiding, this one halted conversation, the tourist now feigning interest in his feet. Together, we moved down our canyon boardwalk in silence.

I knew that I was meant to have chosen more wisely.

The steel planks for this walkway were put in here in 1954.

The first concession stand was built back here in the late 1800s.

The first boat tours are believed to have taken place as early as 1856.

It's going to make you very happy.

—

Storybook Gardens (1956–2010): *WALK THROUGH THE GATES—You look across a pond studded valley to the rolling hills beyond. In this attractive setting you mingle with the old favorites—you come face to face with those storied characters almost forgotten in the rush and hustle of modern living. Here you can—TALK with little Bo-Peep—you'll be surprised and delighted with her stories about sheep. SEE the "Three Men" sailing in their "tub." HEAR the Fiddlers Three, serenading Old*

King Cole. PET the tame goats cavorting with Jack; the Jack of candlestick fame. FEED the Three Little Pigs, marveling the while at their well built brick house. SNAP A PICTURE of that youngster "eating" porridge with the Three Bears. LAUGH with the Happy Clown who dominates the landscape and keeps an eye on things in general. All Roads Lead to Storybook Land where you will find a large paved, free parking lot.

Away from the docks and away from the river, summer heat seeps into the concrete sidewalks and streets that support dozens of souvenir stores, a wedding chapel, countless burger bars, a haunted house, various thrill-oriented museums. Cars and SUVs stop end-to-end, inching forward through lights, their drivers honking horns at other cars carrying other people on other vacations. Here, as elsewhere, garish signs assault and attract the eye. Here, as elsewhere, there are lots and parcels and the latest attempts at luring built up and over and squeezed next to previous attempts, which sometimes need painting or updating. If there's any hum at all it's the panicky hum of consumption, the stress of a Suburban making a left-hand turn, the chatty excitement of children always on the verge of swimming, the irritation of locals trying to get home.

Here, at street level, the divide between local and tourist becomes the easiest distinction to make, simple to turn over in one's hand. In ticket booths, slick-haired youth promise families a savings of 35 percent on a dizzying succession of attractions and, as their clients pay up, calculate the commission they've just made in their heads. Heads of household then look anxiously into one another's eyes as they discuss the offer, one of them returning a wallet to the jeans or purse, a symbol of power now on its unsteady trip home. While the local may cultivate a certain vacancy in the eye, remove herself from her own motions, the tourist will often seize upon this place and do so brick by brick, exclaiming at discoveries in language the detached local has heard a thousand times before. Such divisions can give way to under-the-breath usage of FIB or, from the tourist's point-of-view, assumptions that locals are greedy, insular, and provincial, merely the dull stewards of this, a commercialized playground.

But perhaps this tired distinction also explains the strange appeal of the perversion that played out on the restaurant floor of the old cheese factory. Here I witnessed the microcosmic twist on the usual transaction between the usual characters. This time, bemused locals and near locals purchased something from the strangely vacant insider. In short, it was our turn to be the outsider on a visit, to purchase meekly from people who—though they may not have believed we existed as surely we felt that we must—would nonetheless create and market frosted rooms for us to move around in. Here, I suspect it was my own witlessness that was on display, and so I watched the Endeavor Academy members carefully as they crossed the restaurant floor in funny pants, my chocolate-flavored Coke in hand.

I wonder. How did the words of the Master Teacher affect these warmly humming heads? How is it that these sounds can produce such outward calm? ("Instead of trying to analyze conceptually what you're doing you're letting yourself be what conception is!") Beneath those light and pleasant cake-proffering movements, was there a woman from Escanaba, Michigan, come by the Dodge Neon now for sale outside, a man from Oslo just in by train? Was there a person with a past life now invisible but still sweating, someone still trying to sort through something, sort through nothing, make a new kind of sense? Master Teacher says, "And right now I am well and I am whole and I am here. Let that be the truth if you don't examine it!"

But still, I wonder.

—

"This place is funny," observes the Captain.

Chuck Anderson died in May of 2008 at the age of eighty-three. The man who once told CBS News "I'm going back to heaven. I can leave for heaven at this instant," and that "everybody" was going with him, was survived by hundreds of academy members. They continued to live by the banks of the river, to take my credit card, to return with the slip for me to sign, my first name familiar but my surname etched, temporarily, *Tourist*.

"This place is funny," the Captain says from time to time, habitually, again.

And perhaps what he means is that on the banks of this river, in this occult and commercial town, the act of beckoning crowds to this spot—promising the mere possibility of escape—has very often been enough. What he could also mean is this: the true attraction comes on our penniless day of departure, when crowds finally head home in lines and in silence, their desires still whole but behind them, tangled into the wonder spot's attempt to eddy and alter, into all this gaudiness, all that mercy.

Middle West

He can understand what the "home-folks" in the small towns of the Middle West are talking about.

—1928 usage of "middle west," *Cent. Mag.*,
Oxford English Dictionary

Here, in this heartland, home folks live and farm the earth, their elbows jutting from fields at angles, their sweat dewing the land as far as the eye can see. Here lives a woman with a bosom so ample, so significant, so loose with connotation, her breasts, working entirely on their own, can push a still-baking apple pie right back into that oven, granting that tart fruit some more time to soften. Here, dull practitioners of soil gaze into the distance, their faces filled in with whiteness, their tongues forming around chitchat that refuses to offend, their mouths rounding off vowels into tidy little bits: *Yah. Yah. Oh, yah did? Yah? Oh. Yah. I s'pose so.* This Midwest will take a long time to drive past, its road signs continuously birthing new states: Ohio

Indiana Illinois Michigan Wisconsin Minnesota Iowa Missouri. This land passes, offering itself both as windowed Nowhere and as navigational device, a means of assuring travelers that the long highways on which they wheel themselves are quite rightly blurring them by, heading, that is, in some other direction.

The Midwest, as murky passing referent, also makes possible the kind of punch lines paired with laugh tracks, what Hollywood calls LFNs (laughter from nowhere). Born of the 1950s sitcom, the laugh track consists of the right kind of laughter (nothing spastic, no guffawing) cued at an exact moment for the purposes of aiding the audience in understanding exactly what it is this particular world finds funny. Each perfect laugh of a perfect duration also, and this proves important, perfects the writer's vision, he who can't help himself, he who will hide his smile when each of his jokes lands like a pat on the back. And so a writer at the *Boston Globe* takes a moment, for example, on January 18, 2010, to look in on Fond du Lac, Wisconsin:

WIS. MAN CITED FOR 'ROCKING OUT' TO JOHN DENVER

Police responding to a complaint of loud noise have cited a Fond du Lac man for "rocking out" to the music of John Denver. A police [*sic*] who responded to the man's apartment last week could hear Denver's music through the door. . . .

When asked why he had the music so loud, the man said he was "rocking out."

The Reporter newspaper in Fond du Lac reported that the 42-year-old was cited for unnecessary loud noise. The ticket could result in a fine of about $210.

The late Denver is known for such hits as "Rocky Mountain High" and "Take Me Home, Country Roads."

"Midwest," the writers write, LFN rising up between the lines. Laughter cued, coordinates aligned, this is the where and when of a tidiness running deep. Indeed, the Midwestern man need not appear in Boston long for his rocking out to become both a place and a perpetual action; in minds humming with consciousness all the way up and down the eastern seaboard, Fond du Lac Man continuously rocks out to John Denver, continuously earns himself a citation, and continuously turns back, with an automated swivel of hips, to begin the process all over again. Geographically speaking, this is the making of an island, a way of mapping out impassable waters, willing a neat world to circle up.

—

The Middle West region is oddly named, because the states of Ohio, Indiana, Illinois, Michigan, Wisconsin, Minnesota, Iowa, and Missouri, which make it up, are really neither middle nor west.

—1949 usage of "middle west,"
Oxf. Junior Encycl., Oxford English Dictionary

The island surfaced and then stood, seismic and still dripping, the waters of Lake Superior pouring down its pines. On the map one can see it: the wavering outline of a real-looking island, one that would prove little more than pen jagging mimicked nature onto paper, an island fictitious, made-up, or maybe, just a bit misunderstood. Isle Philippeaux, as it was named, first appeared on a published map in 1744, second in size only to Superior's largest island, the existentially verifiable Isle Royale.

During the century and a half that preceded the island's sudden apparition, French men like Nicolet, Joliet, and Marquette, as well as a number of Jesuits, had shown great pluck and endurance in blundering about this portion of the "New World," wandering up and down rivers, giving names to Indian nations, seeking the souls of humans, the skins of animals, and exploring the contours of the rivers and lakes they named, mapped, renamed, and then mapped again. Nicolet, who believed himself in search of the Northwest Passage, that precious portal to the Orient, is said to have carried across present-day Wisconsin the clothes he would wear when finally he met the Chinese emperor of Cathay. And yet all that erring was more or less long ago by 1744 when Jacques Nicolas Bellin made *Carte des lacs du Canada*, or *Map of Canada's Lakes*. By contrast, this map, in a cartographic moment we might recognize as progress, gives an impression of the accuracy we've come to know. These white men having, at long last, stretched their fingers the entire way around all five of the Great Lakes, inscribed these bodies of water with the names by which we now know them, drawing them in sizes and shapes recognizable to the modern eye.

Though the apparition of Isle Philippeaux came suddenly, without explanation, it nevertheless found its way into the world, even working itself into the Treaty of Paris, signed in 1783, which made of it a reference point—by decree it would sit just south of the border dividing British North America from the United States. Reluctant, perhaps, to shirk such a duty, Phillippeaux stood this ground for a long time, almost an entire century, last appearing on a map in 1842.

From air? Out of lake? Finally, who placed the island there? Bellin, that careful maker of maps, can hardly be a point of origin. Like most mapmakers, he got his information from elsewhere and never scoured the lake for land himself, his work taking place instead at a dry desk with clean plume in hand.

Some historians scrutinize Gaspard-Joseph Chaussegros de Léry and his son of the same name since they likely penned the charts Bellin drew from in making *Map of Canada's Lakes*. But even this pair, who had, in fact, traveled together in New France, gathered their lake map materials from the sketches and assertions of others. And, besides, even if Gaspard-Joseph Junior—apprenticed to his father at only twelve years of age—did the mischievous deed, why wouldn't he have given in to a more useful caprice, naming the island after the baker's teenage daughter, for example, Marie-Thérèse, she who would surely speak to him now? *Je viens de vous créer une isle!* he could have called out to her in the street.

Then there's the fur trader, Louis Denys de La Ronde, a French navy officer who, in 1731, took command of the fur post on Superior's Madeline Island. La Ronde, apparently, had heard Indians tell of copper on Superior's islands and worked out a deal for himself: he'd build a boat and explore all these islands in exchange for nine years of monopolizing the post's trade. If we doubt this character, we'd notice that, as he searched year after year for islands hiding copper deposits, as he moved around that lake, taking what samples he could find, enough islands and inlets and harbors turned up for the purpose of assigning place names that honored his partners and superiors. If we want to believe in his honest mistake, we'd instead remember that he spent much time out there, on his boat, in those vast waters, looking.

It's possible too that the Ojibwe—referred to in the record simply as "the Indians" or "local Indians"—simply needed to find ways of making the burden of possessing native information more rewarding, reciprocal in some way. And so, having known for a long time that some of Lake Superior's islands contained copper, someone told a rapt La Ronde, on the verge of boarding his new vessel, about a ghost woman living on a large island in the middle of those deep waters. This, the informant told La Ronde, was a woman with a bosom so large, so significant, so laden with the copper she formed into medallions, that the clanking layers of her colossal necklace—the size of seven men—succeeded in reflecting every beaming ray of the sun, thus draping this mysterious island of treasure in great darkness. Then, maybe, under the clear light of that day, on a beach with buttered popcorn for all, they sat down to watch him set sail.

Another possibility is that the island decided one day to subsume itself, out of grief, or out of the simple but exquisite irritation at never being found, at a game of hide-and-seek that never showed any mercy.

Another possibility is that the island's still there, swirling away from the scrutiny of satellite images, or permanently ensconced in a rare system of fog so thorough in its efforts to cloud all sense of direction it can render itself, not to mention the land over which it hovers, a fiction.

—

The trouble is that for most Americans the Mid-West, like other regional identities, is less a place on the map than a state of mind.

—1985 usage of "midwest,"
Daily Mail, Oxford English Dictionary

John Denver's "Take Me Home, Country Roads" takes a loose hold of the airwaves, filling the car with its nasal desire for place, this one called West Virginia: "Take me home, country roads / Take me home, now country roads / Take me home, now, country roads." The northbound highway looks dry and hot, the windows have rolled themselves down, and—be still, traveler heart—appearing before us is a summer day and a state of mind, a moment lending itself well to rounding off fictions, to the finding of false islands.

The air from the window waxes poetic, making a masterpiece of each free tendril of hair, and we decide, in that moment of freedom, that it's time to ready our messages. We've worked hard on the words we'd like to leave behind by way of explanation, both for the media who, in a yawning way, might one day attempt to track us, trying to pin this whole story down, as well as for the writers of dictionaries, those abstract persons we love to fret over, praying they'll be meticulous in transcribing our work. We pull in close to fast-food chains and gas stations and place shiny acrylic stickers on exterior walls, gas pumps, and bathrooms doors: "Which Way to the Midwest?" "Middling West and Loving It." "Seeking the Cartographic Truth."

The thrill comes, without a doubt, from pulling away in a clamor of haste, the rubber of the tires peeling off the road, the car squawking, the driver unable to suppress a fist pump. Soon after, there's little but the mechanical hum of the car moving forward plus the pregnant quiet of passengers, explorers who inadvertently dampen maps with the grip of excited hands, explorers whose eyes land on the outside in long and sideways looks, minds on the mapped contours of Isle Philippeaux once again.

The ghost of that island has even written us letters. *You are welcome any time*, she writes in perfect script, *don't call beforehand, just drop by, I make apple pies at the drop of a hat!* And so our mouths water as we imagine the impromptu making of pies that will commence when finally we find her, when, with great effort, we pull our wooden canoe up onto the pebbled beach and climb out, stretching through the smiles and yawns that anticipate, already, the island's great gratitude, the host of secrets to be served up to us on coppery plates.

We're aware of our foolishness, aware we might be disappointed, aware that the Midwest, like many of the earth's places, tilts toward under-imagined and overly caricatured, that it might not be a definite place at all, let alone a concrete navigational direction. And yet we go, hoping we might find something, even imagining for a moment what the signage on the island might look like: "Middle West Passage This Way," the largest arrow will point. Or, "Welcome, Friends, to the Magnetic Midwest." Or, underneath that one, "Site of the Original John Denver Wax Museum."

And so we keep the car rolling. And we go anyway, since we can and because we feel that we must, taking with us the maps that we've made, as well as the irreverence needed to wander over them, lost. In us we keep a tight hold of the desire to scuff that map's straight lines, to mark them momentarily with the traveling imprints of our left foot, Wonder, and our right foot, Doubt. In the end, it's the map's captives, islands made but never seen, that keep us moving, middling, as they say, west.

The Painted Forest

I could have ridden over these ridges and into this valley on the back of a dark gray goat, could have lurched toward the Painted Forest astride a hoofed portent of death. But I arrived instead on wanderlust, my wobbling goat a dented Chevy Cavalier. Here at the beginning, that is, I found everything just as I'd left it. The hills still rose to roll along the spine of the ridge and then fell, tilting into a gentle plunge, a noiseless sweeping. The land still reached up to stand on edge, to halt for a moment the turning of the view before spilling and spreading again, before brushing up the side of another slope, breathless in its effort to make and then gain a good long look of the coming valley. Born here, from this place, I knew how to move across the land, how to be raised up for the purpose of letting go, to be lifted and lowered, gathered and then released: to roll down and then to work my way up again, to the top of the ridge, to the modest view of more hills, to the shortest glimpse of eternity.

I had returned once again to live in Wisconsin and set out to see the places I had not been, to bump into the cobwebs of my home county in hopes that I might find there some mystery once again. I went to the Painted Forest, an old fraternal society hall, because it contained a series of old murals I'd never seen. Geologically, I was in the Driftless area, where North America's glaciers could not reach and thus did not flatten, where the Baraboo River, old as the hills, gathers water as it winds on a dime. I pulled into the tiny town of Valton and parked in front of the white clapboard hall squatting on the sloped edge of town. The Painted Forest, built in 1898, once housed the secret meetings of the local chapter of the Modern Woodmen of America (MWA), one of many fraternal insurance societies. The murals I went in search of, however, were the work of Ernest Hüpeden, an itinerant painter who'd earned his room and board brushing every inch of the hall's interior with the Woodmen's vision, with the stories and symbols of a forest cleared and a future made by men.

When I stepped into this forest for the first time and saw it at first glance, I noticed only the mirroring quality of the mural's depiction of the land. Inside as out, there existed occasional woods or would-be prairie, arching and idyllic fields of vigorous green placed against the relief of blue sky. And yet to walk closer, to enter this painting, was to feel a sudden displacement from what just that moment had felt a familiar scene. Though the hall appeared to be the world in which I'd just been traveling, it ended as a world spiraled by the strange distance between now, this moment of looking, and the year

1899. My Driftless, in other words, had already begun to shift, its hills now holding a man riding a goat, loggers in long pants and white chemises with axes over their shoulders, a log cabin, ritual robes, a bearded patriarch, a great fire.

For what reasons, I wondered, did men once gather here? Was it the secrecy of rituals, the brotherhood of men, the life insurance? What's certain is that the earnestness of the dead, belonging as it does to some other world, risks a future of amused looks from the living. *What strangeness*, I asked, *is this?*

The mural begins in prologue, a man astride a colossal goat whose legs are flung in full gallop, whose fat gray shag bounds from hide into wind. The man's one good arm clutches the spine of the goat while the other swings at the elbow, cradled by a red cloth sling. Hair shooting up wild around him, his mustached mouth opens on a grave panic born of this mix-up in species function, this undomesticated mash-up of creature bodies, the bad path ahead. Forever racing, the goat moves toward the corner of the hall where a tall tree loses its leaves and an owl perches ominously, a human skull and bones piled at its base. As my laminated sheet and interpretive guide explain, "This is a symbol of death."

Even as my eye wanders to ceiling, where a vast sky radiates indifference, this man, the MWA's initiate, continues his gallop, terror leeched to the tips of his hair. I find it difficult to follow the hall's story without once glancing back, to stop thinking about that man on the goat: he who lacks control; he who is doomed to his near-death for eternity. From the beginning, the hall carefully manages its implications, hints at every person's defeat. And while a goat-riding man at first seems surprising or strange, after a while he becomes something else, the cause of a dull thud in the chest, a reminder of a panic gone missing.

Roused by his interest in this, the appearance of a visitor, the ghostly docent Hüpeden springs up in time to help me trace my thoughts. He runs a dry brush along the top of the doorframe, applying a raspy coat, his bristles whisking out the sound of this secret society's most powerful question: *and what / if death should take /* you / *hence?*

Having no answer, I move across a new and merciless land, one whose only allegiances are to tumult and death and time passing. *Face death*, the hall beckons. *Find firmer ground.* I can't help but step in.

—

From the base of the wainscoting to the ceiling, dark shag forest stretches its way up, groaning through ascent. Thick shrubbery twines a stranglehold around tree trunks while the tips of the trees come to arc and lean, white pine placed against clouded sky. In the distance, a forbidding ridge sidles along the horizon, closing the viewer in. Cloistered terrain, untamed wilderness full of danger and death, this is Hüpeden's first full panel. But he has painted in a couple of disparate stumps too, their leveled plain tops swelling from the ground like boastful chests. To chop and beat back, to uproot and plow under, by the late 1800s these acts had a long time been underway. The panel thus leans forward on assertion, on a sense that the taming of this dark forest is exactly where the symbolic life of the modern woodman must begin. Ahead, it says, the hard work of clearing the land.

The Painted Forest's dark green foreboding, the sense of a story being told, leaves me wanting to look at it with something more than undefined suspicion. After visiting the Painted Forest for the first time, I go to the Wisconsin Historical Society Library where my curiosity and I prove altogether common, fraternalism's secrets having long ago generated a history of outsider suspicion. In fact, the orders' secret knowledge and ritual fully anticipated this outsider curiosity, existing as it did to strengthen the difference between those who belong and those who do not. Even this side of a century, this side of the grave, I can smell the must of curtains grown thick on secrets and certainty, a palpable sense of infinite boundary and endless dust.

No doubt the MWA did not often envision its own demise, or the time when its ritual, so elaborate it had to be published in book form, would become available to patrons of the historical library. In the rare books room, under the incongruous glare of fluorescent lighting, I wait for the first edition of *Ritual of the Modern Woodmen of America*, published in 1890, to be delivered to my desk. All around me researchers lose form over books, their craning necks appearing vestigial, as if loss of body were a condition of resurrecting the dead, curiosity the only means of connecting to spirits. Woman, nonmember, when finally I have my chance to open the Ritual, I imagine the hapless protests of Woodmen long ago dead, of founder Joseph Cullen Root. I do not apologize, but I do offer an explanation: *Hüpeden sent me*, I say to them, and then dismiss my own awkwardness, turn the first page.

I learn that no man alive today knows when his day will come, or how his family will survive without him, or what long series of sicknesses and misfortunes might befall him in the interim before death. It is thus wise to join ranks with others, to insure against the worst potentialities. Simply put, a man can approach this dark and frightening world alone—here, where death approaches apace, where the amble of the goat is purely beyond prediction—or he can solicit membership in the Modern Woodmen of America and there grow strong in the stable company of brothers.

In Valton, the time for another man to join has come. The town is settling in, growing quiet. Men slip from crowded homes, propelled into this night by the secrets they're prepared to keep, ascending the steps of Woodman Hall and closing the front door fast behind. The initiate, on the verge of being ushered into mystery, studies the ceiling, wipes a palm on his thigh, then turns his head to hear better what's happening inside. There follows an order hissed, something dragged against wood, then a commotion, all the men moving at once.

The door opens.

The Escort speaks.

"Stranger, having been elected as a member of the Modern Woodmen of America, I presume you have come to this place to seek admission into our camp. Is this your purpose?"

Hüpeden's landscape enfolds in rich blues and greens a crowd of men, placing them against forest. Here travel versions of Valton's men, a farmer, the banker, the blacksmith, and others, their faces locked against admissions of recognizing him. The Ritual instructs: "The hall shall be prepared to represent a miniature exchange or mart of trade. The Neighbors shall wander about the room, converse in low tones with each other, with note-books, money purses and papers in their hands, as if engaged in business transactions and so absorbed in their deals as not to notice Escort and Stranger, unless especially addressed."

Escort: Stranger, we now find ourselves in a miniature busy world. . . . We, in our rags, pass by them unnoticed, for they can see no chance to filch gain from such unpromising beggars as we appear to be. Let us advance to yonder opulent Banker and rehearse a story of suffering and want, and see what reply we will receive.

[To Banker] Sir, can we have a word with you? . . .

Banker: Bosh! What care I for paupers! I pay my taxes regularly, and have, by favorable circumstances and thrift, acquired a competency. If men will die without laying up something for a rainy day, let their widows and progeny suffer. . . . So move on, and do not further waste my valuable time. . . .

Escort: Not even a penny, and we are condemned for the asking! Indeed, this is a cold, unsympathizing world. Selfishness upon every hand; grasping greed and avarice seem to be the instincts that govern mankind. . . . From this experience, how fearful the contemplation of the future becomes. . . .

[To Adviser] Worthy Adviser, we seek knowledge of the Arcana, or mystery, that enables the worthy man in rags, who earns his daily bread by the sweat of his brow, to provide for a rainy day, and especially for his loved ones, if death should take him hence.

> **Adviser:** Truly spake the Patriarch when he said: "Man is born to trouble as the sparks fly upward." . . . Organization is the breath to the life of culture and progress; out of this idea nations have been evolved, and the university, the school, and a multitude of humane enterprises have come to benefit the people. Then, Strangers, the Arcana which I have to reveal is this: Go straightaway and be adopted as Neighbors in the Camp of the Modern Woodmen, and your fears shall dissipate like the morning vapors.

The Golden Age of Fraternity welcomed a great many men in this way, with order and symbols and frequent allusions to death. Fraternal life insurance orders alone included an estimated 1.3 million members by 1890 and 8.5 million by 1910. And by 1908, the most popular societies had distributed more than $1 billion in benefits. *Everybody's Magazine*, a general interest magazine of that time, offered its sense of this phenomenon, calling the nation's legions of fraternal orders an "enormous army" made up of "the middle-class workman, the salaried clerk, the farmer, the artisan, the country merchant, and the laborer." Together, they worked "to insure their helpless broods against abject poverty. Rich men insure in the big companies to create an estate; poor men insure in fraternal orders to create bread and meat. It is an insurance against want, the poorhouse, charity, and degradation."

And so our initiate, his life ground down by private worry, his bones weary from improvising manhood, or survival, or both, offers himself up for adoption. His spine lengthens. His shoulders drop. Never mind those fears of falling, of the children someday floundering, of the family left behind, now he is nerved for greater endeavors, made strong by a brotherhood in which all members are equal, in which everyone insures everyone against the most monumental failure of all.

—

The Painted Forest closed for the winter and yet my mind kept returning to peer into the Woodmen's promise. I was attempting to fix the Painted Forest—in place, in time—imagining that if I came to understand it, then I'd be, in some way, a trespasser in the fold. This is how, as I was granting the source of my curiosity a place at the center of the universe, the world really did move beneath me, everything shifting toward something else, until my imagined narrative—me, the stranger in a strange land—merged with the present and I awoke from my research long enough to realize what had been bringing me here this whole time.

When I had gone in search of books in the basement stacks, a political war that had been brewing for years had finally broken out far above. Neighbors were turning on neighbors, on school teachers and other public employees, people with health insurance and pensions, because this was meant to save an economy not so long ago sunk by a lawless band of the very rich. Half of Wisconsin stopped to protest. The other half, some of whom were struggling to hang on to homes or jobs, cheered. And because these new politics depended on no one listening and everyone yelling, on a sharpened practice of ideological bloodletting, at family gatherings that spring, people simply stopped speaking, turning hot dogs over backyard fires to the sound of the safest of repetitions, the one about how very long spring had taken to come.

That winter I wore myself out on protest, rushing to the capitol with each new development, screaming to the beat of drums, sending pizzas to the people on the nights I wanted to go home. But I also spent time below, in the library's basement stacks, mixing my worlds, drawing strength from obscure places. "Organization," the woodman proclaims (with characteristic awkwardness), "is the breath to the life of culture and progress; out of this idea nations have been evolved, and the university, the school, and a multitude of humane enterprises have come to benefit the people."

In the stacks, dry heat roaring through metal vents, I scribbled my notes, caught in a cobweb of my own making. Above ground, in the light of day, I despaired, wondering what would become of us.

—

Hüpeden lived half his life in other people's homes, barns, and storage rooms, earning temporary room and board in exchange for painting a prized place or flower or homestead onto wood, bottle, mattress material, and even canvas tarp.

In *Burch-Bolden Family Homestead*, painted in 1906 and held now by the Wisconsin Historical Society, a daughter clad in dress and large brimmed hat runs down the path from white farmhouse to road, rushing to wave at the carriage containing the mother and father who, just then, return home. The boy, a son, walks along the road with his dog, a stick thrown over his shoulder as he embarks on a chore or an expedition of his own invention.

Behind curtains, from the vantage point of distant barns, Hüpeden woke to the morning routine of other families, saw a girl often ebullient, a boy too often disappearing into imaginary lands, parents for whom his work was most agreeable when it bathed the homestead or its ambition in prosperity. And so Hüpeden, known locally as "the bum painter," painted while perambulating, his American life a decades-long exercise in finding and stirring each family's secret heart and then moving on, saying his goodbyes before the welcome soured.

Born in Germany, Hüpeden arrived to New York harbor in 1878. More than twenty years later, sometime in 1898, he walked into this valley, arriving just as the local camp of the Modern Woodmen of America was completing construction on their meeting hall. His biography comes complete with a myth passed from one generation to the next, a legend in casual making: In Germany, Hüpeden was educated in several universities and worked as a bank teller. After a false accusation of embezzlement, he was imprisoned for a term of seven or eight years. Given paints and a brush, there he taught himself to paint. But when the real perpetrator of the crime made a deathbed confession, a newly freed Hüpeden set sail for America, fleeing the German militarism he often decried and leaving behind a wife and child from whom he'd become estranged. And yet Lisa Stone, art professor and art environment specialist, notes that the manifest of the *Herder*, the ship Hüpeden boarded in Hamburg in 1878, lists his approximate age as twenty, a detail casting doubt on the possibility of his seven-year imprisonment and suggesting that what Hüpeden fled might have really been Germany's eight-year military conscription.

Shortly after Hüpeden walked into the lively town of Valton, he was commissioned to paint a mural depicting the Battle of Manila Bay for the Woodman Hall's stage. The Woodmen were so pleased with his work they asked him to paint the rest of the hall too. He completed his masterwork over the next two years, boarding in the local hotel and then in a backroom of the post office. And though Woodland Township, in which Valton is situated, has the unusual distinction of being dry, and the Woodmen themselves lauded temperance, Hüpeden was not of a similar ilk. Through accounts both blithe and condemnatory, we everywhere learn that he had a so-called moral failing, a love of drink lifted from his person by wagging tongues, salvaged over and over again by and for the historical record. The cause of his death could have been drink, but winter also had a hand. On December 8, 1911, in nearby Hub City, Webster Leatherberry went out to his buggy shed and discovered Hüpeden's frozen body.

Other details have the simplicity of a thing worn smooth and uncomplicated over time, and so make a spare sketch of Hüpeden's transience: his clandestine book borrowing and voracious reading, his suspected tallness. He is survived also by "quiet" and "thoughtful," by "kind" and "funny," by a haphazard eulogy that summons who he might have been before Charity came to place him in a pauper's grave, his epitaph not death but dependence, his unmarked plot an unrelenting shame.

—

Below the ground, in the dim light of the olive-colored stacks, I continued to track the mysteries of a secret society. To view *The Painted Forest* once, I realized, was to find comedy in its contradictions, to feel faintly smug for having witnessed the quaint simplicity of the dead. To linger longer, however, means reversing that power relation: now it is you, member of the self-satisfied living, who has missed the point. Fraternalism's evocation of opposites, what historian Ann Clawson, in her book *Constructing Brotherhood: Class, Gender, and Fraternalism*, calls its "symbolic resolution of conflicts," was not the accident of men living blind to their present but a significant and purposeful part of fraternalism's appeal. The Painted Forest had been the ground on which the irreconcilable was reconciled via elaborate ritual and joining, a place for the man feeling plagued by competing identities and a changing world to hang up his many hats and enter an alternate and equalizing land.

Here stands the symbol of mystical forest and here its woodman, a man made strong by brotherhood. Here, where opposites can abound, the woodman is loyal to his own single-handed triumph, to his own lonely right to axe and land, while remaining unwavering in his belief in mutual aid, the strength of his brotherhood, the "idea of organization." In other words, the woodman espouses fidelity to the group, takes part in its collective insurance plan, goes to his window to discover his Neighbors putting in his oats, but still retains the American man at the root of his own individualist making; he still gets to prosper, it would seem, for having yanked up his own bootstraps. Even the ritual he enacts at his regularly scheduled meetings gradually ceases expounding on the interdependency of all men, singing instead the praises of the order's strength and innovation—fraternalism as a single unstoppable force, a means of propelling America into industrial greatness, the most natural extension of the individual man's will to prosper.

In entering this forest, the woodman, regardless of trade or occupation, is also granted the privilege of arriving equal to all men. Here, he will socialize with men of all classes. Though an alluring and popular characteristic of fraternalism, this too is not entirely what it seems. In practice of course, the MWA operates on exclusion. Men choose their newest brother, membership skewing no doubt toward the upright and socially upstanding, toward those not newly arrived in the country, toward men who already have some power within their communities. Black men are barred from joining the MWA, their presence a strain on otherwise easy feelings of brotherhood. However, the oft-replicated fraternal model is far less exclusive than the native white orders it spawns. In this, the "Golden Age of Fraternity," black men as well as ethnic and immigrant groups simply form their own exclusive organizations. The order's brand of equality poses yet another irony. Focusing on every man's mortality turns out to be easy, its politics being that of curbing politics, discouraging any recognition of difference.

The business of brotherhood is yet another contradiction held to the heart of the order. At the Head Camp in Illinois, men are charged with scratching mathematical equations onto the applications of potential members—How long might this one live? How much might he pay in?—imposing restrictions on membership in the name of curbing financial risk. He cannot join if his profession is dangerous. He cannot join if he is over forty-five years of age, or in poor health. And yet at the same time, fraternal leaders rail against the callous profanity that is the commercial insurance industry. Insurance, they maintain, should be based on brotherhood, never business. That fraternal organizations compete for members and expand via paid recruiters somehow also doesn't seem to undermine the orders' professed reason for being what Clawson calls "a relation of brotherhood established by ritual and free from the demands of the marketplace."

To the Woodmen, fraternal insurance is special insurance, a mutual aid made especially for men. This explains why fraternal organizations are among the most vocal opponents to the campaign for compulsory health insurance proposed in America in the 1910s. Faced with their potential irrelevance, legions of fraternal orders double down on their own sectarian mode of collectivization. Fraternal insurance, as they see it, is self-insurance, and thus superior in nature. This is a form of self-help granted men by a God who made America for the express purpose of testing them, a God who had reserved for men the singular responsibility of extracting triumph from a once distant and difficult land. "True manhood obtains through contest," or so says John Sullivan, Modern Woodman, as he addresses the National Fraternal Congress in 1918 on the threat of social insurance.

In the end, the forest is alive with tensions. The woodman's symbols and rituals exist for the purposes of resisting final interpretation, moving forever between concealment and revelation and achieving the kind of polyvalence that keeps the woodman in solace and searching. Mystery, then, is mythically indispensable, a balm that makes tidy work of fraternalism's affair with opposites. Through ritual and its attendant mystery, the woodman manages to garner a momentary control over the problems of life and death, capitalism and community, wealth and poverty, the past and the present. And so *The Painted Forest*, in its attempt to seize a vision, to fix a world that was always going to turn, seems to settle things.

Go straightaway and be adopted . . . your fears shall dissipate like the morning vapors.

And yet one hundred years later, the force of a separate contradiction, this one inadvertent and uncontained, still haunts The Painted Forest, bringing to the hall some suggestion of the life outside its reach. The brush of a bum painter touched every wooden fiber of this place, exchanging itself on commission, filling the hall with tension. *We / in our rags / pass by them / unnoticed*, Hüpeden painted and seems to paint still, made present by his absence, by what we don't know of what he thought about all this, the surest of futures to come.

—

Hüpeden's next full panel unnerves and offends, its dark and half denuded slopes managing to suggest that all life gets willed down with this force, that the place where the ridges dump everything is the place we'll all end up. And here, where the earth all but bottoms out, is where the woodmen do their hazing, where they've tied an initiate to a stake and begun terrorizing him with black masks on their faces. Smoke rises behind him, fire blazes about him, his face bears a cartoonish frown. Surrounding the initiate, uniformed woodmen in masks tend the fire with spears while outside the ring more black-masked members drag men in plain dress toward the flames. Though the scene may be borrowed from the initiation ritual of another all-white fraternal order, the Improved

Order of Red Men, no amount of background scrapes away its implications. Here black faces are worn to evoke the symbolic terror of the MWA initiate. Here a dark and dangerous forest and a fear of racial difference connect in a most confident way and the "forest" takes the initiate prisoner, latching him tight to his powerlessness.

The Ritual, far from finished with the Ceremony of Adoption, begins testing the initiate's mettle as well. Since fraternal orders needed to recruit and retain their bases, which meant providing both entertainment and a system of morality and mutual aid, fraternal rituals began to accommodate the change in middle class notions of masculinity that were occurring at the turn of the century. Though once the test of any man, or the Victorian man, had lay in his ability to be dignified at all times, now a white middle-class man was expected to help create a culture of horseplay, a culture where, as historian William D. Moore describes it in his article "Riding the Goat: Secrecy, Masculinity, and Fraternal High Jinks in the United States, 1845–1930," "physical toughness, composure, [and] humor" reigned. A stiff and neatly pressed dignity gave way to the ability to laugh at one's self, to be jocular *and* composed. And this is how later editions of the Ritual come to place the initiate onto the back of a goat powered by the zeal of members pushing it from behind.

Until the turn of the twentieth century, the fraternal goat had been merely an abstraction, a symbol of secrecy. Confused outsiders, unaware of the content of fraternal rituals or their meaning, knew only that, somehow, quite curiously, a goat was involved. And then, as Moore explains, "the goat, previously a purely literary or artistic device, assumed concrete three-dimensional form." DeMoulin Bros. & Co. of Greenville, Illinois, describe their popular product "The Rollicking Mustang Goat":

> The eccentric front wheel serves as a safeguard against the candidate taking a "header" but does not rest on the floor except when "Billy" takes a notion to buck. Then the handle-bar is raised until the frame runs on all three wheels. As the hubs are out of center, the irregular motions produced are indeed very realistic and characteristic of the goat family. The peculiar arrangement of wheels and the strong spiral spring pivoted to the body, together with the up-and-down motion of the handle-bar, produce the desired results.

With DeMoulin's top-of-the-line "Ferris Wheel Coaster Goat," the initiate rides a goat mounted at the center of a wheel roughly seven feet in diameter. Just as he begins to think the ride is easy enough—the goat holding steady as the wheel moves around him—the wheel flips him upside down, the holsters on his feet presumably preventing him from crashing on his head. "The firing of a blank cartridge adds to the consternation," the catalog explains. "A ba-a-a attachment also makes this goat more goaty."

The goat and his ilk remind the initiate that he is not master of himself, not really, that Death and disaster await him, that the task before him is to gain control by finding

humor in his own lack of control, to never grant the group his humiliation. And for his willingness to make some fun that night, he is offered the balm of brotherhood. "All in good fun," is what they might say, though that expression has long been busy with defending itself, with pretending there's nothing more to be said.

In a Currier & Ives print from 1887 entitled *Initiation Ceremonies of the Darktown Lodge*, the racist caricature of a black man attempts to ride a goat in a fraternal hall strewn with chaos and disorder. This is comical for putting the wrong man in the wrong place, for the mayhem that ensues when fraternal boundaries are transgressed and the apparatus of control falls into the wrong hands. Only certain men, the Woodmen know, can ride the goat and manage the chaos of death. Only certain men can access this version of self-reliance.

"I don't know when I'm going to die!" nonmembers yell from atop the goat, but their exclamations land like violations before crawling in long silence to the hall's front door, they and their fears now wandering the hills on their own, limping west, each toward their own setting sun.

—

The large back wall of *The Painted Forest* faces north, marking our arrival, symbolizing our embrace. The wise patriarch, enveloped in gray robe, long white hair and beard, takes the plain-clothed initiate by one hand toward a campfire while pointing to the distance with the other, to an imposing castle built high on a stark gray mountain, Hüpeden's depiction of the MWA lodge. From the castle's towers fly three flags: one the U.S. flag; one billowing the words "Peace, Light, Safety"; the last inscribed "MWA Valton Camp No. 6190." Jovial, uniformed Woodmen follow the patriarch and initiate along, axes thrown over their shoulders, heads turned as if in casual conversation with one another, this ambiance of wisdom and acceptance something they have long ago come to enjoy. The patriarch's eyes have slid sideways, his gaze casting back and down, to study with great seriousness the face of the initiate, he who encounters the Arcana for the first time, his eyes wide, his cheeks flushed.

The Ritual thus erupts in official welcome. The secret handshake is imparted, but also the Working Sign, the

Woodmen's Sign, the hand test, the grip, and the secret rap on the hall door. There are the working tools of the camp and their symbols—the beetle for industry, the axe for power, the wedge for progress. The initiate is also instructed in the Recognition Sign (a way of knowing a woodman from another camp), the Warning Sign (in shorthand noted as "I-H-L-T-B-C!"), and the Woodmen's Honors. The reason for choosing the woodmen identity is even explained: "The trembling leaves and waving boughs of the monarchs of the forest, that have braved the tempests for many score of years, fill our hearts with admiration. There they stand, ready for the hand of the woodman to prepare them for practical use in the world's economy." Here then are some secrets: the beetle, axe, and wedge.

—

In the 1915 edition of the Woodmen's ritual, Death also makes an appearance. Concealed behind a curtain for nearly the entire length of the adoption ceremony, he suddenly steps in front of the escort and initiate to speak in a "hollow sonorous monotone."

> **Death:** I am Death! Relentless and unsparing! I visit the cradle and take the smallest of humanity, leaving the mother to wail and mourn. The strongest of men are crushed beneath my blow. . . . I strike where I like, when I please, and whom I desire. . . . *(Raising hand as though to strike.)*

Escort: *(Speaking quickly.)* Stay, O Death. Withhold your hand! Strike not this Stranger. We are on our way to protect his home. If you demand his life now his loved ones will be objects of charity.

Death: Withhold my hand? Who are you to make such a demand? . . . Yesterday, last week, or last year, you could have done these things and have made provision for those dependent upon you. What excuse have you to offer for your neglect?

Escort: None, O Death, except that we did not realize its necessity until yesterday, and today we are on our way to seek protection. . . .

Death: Upon your earnest pleas, I will relent and let you pass this time. But, mark you well! Be ready when next I come. No excuse will then serve to dissuade me from my purposes. It may be early. It may be late. It may be in youth, manhood, or old age; you know not when. But come I will, so be prepared! *(Retreating.)* Be prepared! Be prepared! *(Disappears.)*

Charles Braiden Gibeaut, gone in 1901, was "a farmer from the ground up" and the first of the seventeen Valton men whose deaths prompted an MWA benefit claim. A charter member and the father of ten or more children, Charles served as assessor for the Township of Woodland for five terms, chairman for four terms, treasurer for three terms, and then, in 1900, he ran for Sauk County Register of Deeds. A promotional newspaper article from this time calls him "one

of the most popular men in Sauk County" and boasts: "He has always attended strictly to business and during the past thirty years has not been out of the Sauk County limits more than sixty days, all told." His sepia-toned portrait also hangs in the entryway to the Painted Forest. In it, the smooth skin of a man appearing barely into his forties frames small, lightly upward-cast eyes. His hair has just begun to recede and his chin and ears thin into agile pointedness. One senses wiry shoulders beneath that heavy black suit, some oil worked into the round black tuft of hair at rest on his forehead, bottomless resolve in his heavily winged mustache.

In 1896, his wife Sophia gave birth to what seems to have been their eighth child, a boy named Royal Forest. Whether the name's congruity with MWA lore was coincidental or the result of fraternal enthusiasm I cannot know, but Charles joined the MWA in the same year. And little Royal Forest does figure in Hüpeden's next panel, the only wall to incorporate a stock MWA image. Here, a homestead cabin is nestled into woods that are, that moment, being felled by three woodmen with axes. A woman stands back in the cabin's doorway holding her babe and watching the men at work, the foreground studded with stumps. Royal Forest, a boy of two or three stands small and eager, watching the men from amid chopped logs, the felling motion of their many axes insuring his young life against want.

In 1901, less than two years after Hüpeden finished *The Painted Forest*, Charles Gibeaut left this world with most of his children still in it, an insurance policy ready to be paid in his name. One of the most upstanding men in all of Sauk County, his death gathered a dedicated group of mourners, none of whom talked about the shock of it nor the injustice, repeating instead *His wisdom, His will*. But his casket was also trailed by admiration for this, a man who did not rely on Charity to make provisions for this day. A man who, in his last moment, did not need to locate his panic or regret what he had not done because already he'd made a firm practice of greeting Death, had done it a hundred times. And there in front of all the others, his body without life, he remained, somehow, still in possession of that day. Curious the way the living then found themselves taking orders from the dead, the way Gibeaut had half escaped Death by insuring even his own redemption. This,

the Neighbors avowed by marking his grave, by following the script, is the Modern Woodman.

The Ritual finally done, the woodmen now linger on atmosphere and goodbyes, step under the portrait of Charles Braiden Gibeaut, and pass into the night once again. The Escort, he who shepherded a new Neighbor into the Camp this evening, gazes at stars as he walks back to the small house he shares with his wife at the other edge of town. He thinks of her there and imagines her asleep, her slim body at rest but still anticipating the weight and arrival of his own beside her. He feels that he might walk this night as if on a swell, that maybe he joined his wife hours ago and there began to dream of this, a short journey home. The night air anonymously ushers him forward but the stars seem to take a special interest, touching him over and again with a single question, *And what of you, Vilas Eastman? What of you?* He hears his footsteps but they sound like those of some other mortal, a man meaning nothing to him, and so he shivers. He must continue to pay his fee.

Of that, he's certain.

—

In *The Painted Forest*'s depiction of the future, the year is 1999. A horse-drawn wagon hustles down a Main Street whose peach-brown boardwalks stretch back to a vanishing point. In the future, Valton's prosperity seems to unfurl forever, brick and mortaring itself across the heart of county and nation. Washed in yellow or erected in red and brown brick, the storefronts bear Woodmen names and feature a mercantile goods store, a "Hotel de Gibbons," a business marked "Hardware." White awnings line businesses. An American flag flies high over the town. A few men assemble outside a business marked "Saloon," a detail once characterized as Hüpeden's inside joke. And in the foreground, a cut out of the bank reveals a widow clothed in black inside. She holds an insurance policy for $2,000 as she smiles at the window of a teller who turns sideways, pleased to be drawing money from the drawer. Another teller, standing at the window to the right, places his hands wide on the counter, leans back slightly so that he too might cast an approving smile down on this scene.

Here, on the occasion of exultance, at the first breath of its finale, *The Painted Forest* provokes displacement once again. Its story, contained by walls made of beginning, middle, and end, reaches now for the outside world, for the way things will one day be, and there it twists and cracks. From the door, I hear the intermittent sound of pickup trucks motoring past on the highway that might have become "Main," en route to the super store of some bigger town.

Hüpeden's final panel faces the unbridled forest in which Death was imminent and danger a certainty, where the forest needed chopping, where the vulnerable initiate first considered his individual risk. Here, on the other end of the Woodmen's vision, just past the Valton of 1999, a beautiful landscape showcases the mastery of men, a forest now made civil and welcoming. Delicate red, white, and blue flowers dapple the foreground of the frame, approaching a pleasantly uniform size and shape, but then soon give way to a vast opening of smooth green carpet rolling back into the horizon. Bushes line the perimeter of this open space where deciduous trees, including white birch, rise to fill the air in tilting welcome, the entire scene a sort of gentle greeting. Half-standing stumps, symbols of collective progress, are cradled by scenery, appearing in the middle where the eye cannot miss them or their point about legacy, about what has been made and by whom.

From the vantage point of 2003, Jason Kaufman—self-described nonjoiner and historical and cultural sociologist—writes witheringly of groups like the MWA in his book *For the Common Good? American Civic Life and the Golden Age of Fraternity*, scratching out another legacy for fraternalism: "the rise of a fragmented political system based around social interests rather than common interests," and the reason "America missed its primary opportunity to join western Europe in the adoption of people-friendly social policies." The fraternal insurance order offered self-protection but also, Kaufman suggests, "self-segregation and self-aggrandizement."

Not everything, the Woodmen insisted, can be assessed according to the criteria of the market. *Not my life, not his*, they said, as they gathered together in half defiance in lodges at nighttime, or built tuberculosis hospitals, or pooled money for a member that moment in need. *Not my life and not his,* said the men of Camp 6190, proudly protecting their own, readying this legacy for our long admiration.

—

We / in our rags / pass by them / unnoticed, Hüpeden painted for the Woodmen, for the pleasure of so much canvas, for the ease of sleeping inside, his full belly an animal curled beside him in bed. Now asleep, his future ghost, another self, slips off to enact *The Painted Forest*'s undoing, to brush it back toward undone. Valton, he notices now, did not boom so much as retract, most everyone gone off to seek security somewhere else. So he paints broad white strokes over the last panel until the old painter watching this from behind a veil of sleep and a hundred years of dust turns from left shoulder to right, emits an anguished groan. All night, he paints by the light of three candles, a fitful Hüpeden straining to see the work, to apprehend from beneath the weight of deep, departing sleep the nature of his own revision, the future as it comes.

As Valton's patch of earth turns to daylight, to the beginning of a hundred years gone by, the Woodmen vision wakes up broken, its resolution, once etched out of fear and night, undone by the work of Hüpeden's ghost, by the simple fact of intervening years, by a future seeded with new strangers and doubt. In the last panel's place, Hüpeden's most beautiful landscape yet appears lined in thick brown bordering marking it as separate. The view here is vast, the visibility unrealistic. Distant hills seem to rise and roll along the spine of a ridge and then fall, tilting into a gentle plunge, a noiseless sweeping. They reach up, stand on edge, still for a moment the long run of the view before spilling and spreading again, before brushing up the side of another slope, breathless in their effort to make and then gain a good long look of the coming valley.

And yet with a closer look it becomes clear that these distant hills do not rise up all alone, that their summits and slopes are spotted with potter's fields, with crude brown caskets buried unevenly, crammed into awkward slivers of earth. The eye drops also to the lower right-hand corner, where deep in a plunging hollow Hüpeden has placed a mud colored casket and signed it with his name, his epitaph nothing more than a map of unmarked graves, a hundred old lives revealed.

—

When I emerge one day the following summer from the dark and dusty coolness of the Painted Forest, from its acrid smell of a hundred years gone by, I cross through a doorway flush with afternoon light and come upon Valton one year on. Absent is the burgeoning city built upon brotherhood. Here instead is a town just barely, about a dozen homes, two churches, five streets, a cemetery, and everywhere the absence of families long ago moved on. Apart from leaves, apart from grasses twining in the wind, nothing and no one stirs. Even the hills, their underbellies lined in caskets, pose mid-tumble.

And yet outside the Painted Forest, outside the reach of its omniscience, an odd mystery still pours through clear bright light, revealing a Driftless that did not shift, that has barely altered at all. Sleepy Valton, though a shadow of what once was, can still stir up the same question, hanging the Woodmen legacy on the blue blankness of a perfect afternoon: *and what / if death / should take /* you */ hence?*

Out on the land, in the distance, the Stranger thinks she makes out log cabins squatting into forest and hillside and shivers. She scrambles to her car but finds it wet with paint, the dark gray image of a rollicking goat painted across the driver's side door, and here she shivers again. *Not everything,* she utters, digging in, *can be assessed according to the criteria of the market*! as if this pronouncement, her individual resistance, will find for her an alternative to panic and retreat. In her goat she attempts to roll away from the ghosts of a story still trying to being told, but even as she is lifted to the rise of a ridge and lowered again, she cannot find release, not from the tenuous nature of her own self-reliance and not from an America in need. "This," the laminated sheet and interpretive guide explains, "is a symbol of death."

She rolls down hillsides that hold to their slopes the blackest of soil, and then works her way up again, to the top of the ridge, to the modest view of more hills, to yet another short glimpse of eternity.

Everybody Comes 'Round Here

A retelling of "Victoria Wisconsin Peck Hawley (Lately Interviewed)," written by O. D. Brandenburg for the *Madison Democrat*, reprinted in *A Standard History of Sauk County, Wisconsin*, in 1918

Even now, Victoria Wisconsin Peck Hawley, First White Child Born, attracts visitors. Schoolgirls and history buffs come to kneel before the prospect of her pioneer remembrances: about Maw and Paw climbing the Baraboo Bluffs so as to stumble into an unsettled valley, about the few coarse comforts of a log cabin in winter, about any memory with the texture of unground wheat. Snow drifting onto quilts heaped onto human sleep, the queer and close scent of a body's longtime oil, fathers falling from wagons and snapping their necks (the animal sound of their ugly deaths), but also the wild honey and the wild berries, which were in more pleasant days everywhere to be found.

Born in 1837, the same year the Winnebago, or Ho-Chunk, were officially cheated of their land, Victoria would become a living historical marker, a tiny-bodied harbinger of widespread settlement to come. Probably no one explained it to her right away, "This, baby Victoria, is the Territory of Wisconsin, and you, one of the first all-white children to be born in it." She would have to sit up and ascertain this point later, noticing that her wailing seemed to have carried for miles, that the high-pitched honk of her squawking had signaled to white men that the time and place were ripe for homesteading, that any man could now make a life from this land, any man could now prosper.

Almost eighty years later, in August of 1917, Victoria Wisconsin Peck Hawley lives with her second husband in a summer cottage near Mirror Lake. Mrs. Hawley, nervous, demented, darts about during Madison journalist O. D. Brandenburg's visit. Brandenburg sits on the porch attached to their one-room dwelling and tries not to imbue his unbiased report with the disappointment of a man who's traveled sixty miles for this. This Mrs. Hawley, she of advanced age and deteriorating mind, is claiming that all Maw's precious books and papers, records of the family's earliest settlement, have been lost, taken, that is, to Omaha in a trunk. Her husband, twenty years her junior, interjects so that he might quietly clear things up. "We didn't lose any books," he tells the journalist.

Summer wanes and so, Brandenburg notes, the thin walls of the Hawley's cottage have already begun to look foolish, the entire situation ill-arranged. Indeed, the state of Mrs. Hawley's mind coupled with the coming winter have all but soured the whole story, which was meant to fill two columns, which was meant to have something to do with rooting down, about origin stories scraped whole from a new land, not about transience, not about the disjunctions of a pioneer without memory, the homesteader without home.

Maw's books and papers, Mrs. Hawley insists several times, aren't even here in this cottage, having been taken to Omaha far away from here. There, out of reach and out of context, the local treasure that might have been, remains unopened, closed against the indifference of a new and different county. Possibly there had been little to find at all. "Sunny today, very dry," Roseline Peck might have recorded once in a hand only she could decipher before getting up to punch her bread loaves, salt her hams.

"My maw was born in Vermont and Paw in New York," Mrs. Hawley tells Brandenburg. "Everybody comes 'round here picking up things. Even some schoolgirls were here, and they got it that Maw was a squaw, but she wasn't. The papers have had a lot of stuff about us, but all the reporters know is what they are told by those who know nothing."

"And when did your mother die?" Brandenburg inquires, pen in hand.

"I swan, I forget!" Mrs. Hawley replies. "I shall be glad when it is all over and I am gone too. Maw and I once went down to the Madison state fair and an old Irishwoman came out of a house and said, 'I was the first white child born in Madison,' and Maw said, 'You were, were you?' ha-ha." Then the tiny woman disappears from the room only to re-enter again: "Hawley there is a late settler. He don't know anything."

But it is the late settler's congenial talk of old times that at long last offers Brandenburg his pearl: Mr. Eben Peck, Victoria's father, once led his family from Madison into the Baraboo Valley where they were among the first to stake a claim. It would seem, however, that life on this particular frontier could not last forever, the frontier being a scythe that could not stop sweeping west. By 1844, by the time Mr. Peck had finished work on some outbuildings, he took a look around and found himself an established and unmoving member of the middle. And so he abandoned his wife, daughter, and son in the valley and headed west. Up to the time of the reporter's visit, up to that very moment in fact, the local record showed no more sign of Eben Peck except to say that he'd died on the Plains at the hands of Indians, the kind of epilogue once fixed to the lives of men who had disappeared.

And yet, as it would turn out, Eben Peck did write, sending at least three letters from California. And in them he suggested he'd like to come back, to which an indignant Mrs. Peck replied that he could stay right where he was. "He was in the honey business in California and wanted to sell honey to his son Victor, who was then running the eating house at the West Madison depot in Madison. The children would not allow him to come back either," Hawley says.

Having collected, at least, this supplement to the extant record, Brandenburg takes up his pad of paper and pen, bids them both goodbye, gives Mrs. Hawley the worst of his brightly numbing smiles, and then steps out of the summer cottage in which soon, he is quite sure, they will both be shivering. Back at his heavily oiled desk in Madison, he types out his ending on deadline: "I called at this humble abode hoping to obtain an interview late in life from the first white child born in Madison, but I had come too late!" Exit Brandenburg.

And so Eben Peck, early settler, perpetual wanderer, did not perish on the Plains, but lived long past that particular prairie, far beyond that Midwestern settlement. Having followed the frontier until it ran out of earth, having filled his eyes on ocean, he moved side to side, and then, ever moving, always shifting, he began to think back. "Perhaps the depot could use some good honey? I'll sell it at the fairest possible price," Eben wrote. "Even without the sale of honey, I have half a mind to come on back." And later, he'd waxed nostalgic, "Remember how we woke to snow on the blankets? I think of it often, Roseline." Maw reads over the last letter once more—"I never forget the time of it we had coming over those hills, not a clearing in place"—before dropping all three letters into the stove, stringing her wash over the quick flash of their heat.

Everybody comes back here. Even Eben now writes from California, taking his half step back, reimagining the land so that he might find it once again, so that he might feel, one more time, that all the world is a beginning, an origin story in which he is the tale and the telling, in which he is the person who can come upon all new things rightly. Didn't wee Victoria once fall into the cream? Didn't the bears sometimes cause such a fright? And remember the winters, the illness, the death? Forgive me, Roseline, Eben pleads, but aren't I the one to tell it? Wasn't I Eben Peck, the First One of that valley?

"I shall be glad when it is all over," Victoria calls into the air of her visitors, plying the bones of her hand to the doorknob, readying herself to bid all of it goodbye. First White Child Born, she will jerk the flimsy door of her summer cottage shut, attempting to cast to the wind what was once the long, definite line of a certain kind of longing, the breadcrumbs of a story that kept bringing everyone back to claw for roots, turnips, ash, to be the one now doing the digging.

"Paw!" Victoria will yell, laughing, incredulous, when her cottage door seems to rattle with one last knock, "There ain't no Indians here!" What follows will be chronicled in more modern papers, how time has battered the visitor's old dreams, which he'd staked like scores to be settled in front of what remained of Victoria's door, this slim winter ruin the lone heat of a future still made for men, still keen on pioneers.

Animals

In the very beginning I spent time hoping that the baby would be human and not squirrel or, as I legitimately feared, possum. Why wouldn't or couldn't my uterus, an organ lined in risk and chance, twist the signal, cradle the curled body of something else? The embryo of a possum really could have been the one seizing from inside me what little food I swallowed, extracting enough force from soda crackers and grapefruit to thicken its spine and strengthen the battering of its own heart, growing, in other words, big and biological, astounding but scientifically certain. Was there any shape—of body or thought—that my nausea could not accommodate, could not twist and fold? *No*, I insisted, steadying myself on spinning earth, *there was not*.

I kept coming upon turned or twisting thoughts, finding them in every tucked away place, in the smells that sprang from the mouth of the fetus's father, in the putrid depths of the wool balaclava that gripped my face as I gagged my way to work in the cold. Everything blurred. Everything sharpened. Either I was growing an animal inside of me or I was immersed in the prolonged haze of very slowly realizing I'd always been one myself. I had trouble figuring out which. In making eye contact with neighborhood dogs, I could see that I smelled all that they smelled—between us passed blasé looks of species recognition—and so I wondered if all along I hadn't been one of the greatest and most elaborate of fools, an animal who washed and wore clean underwear; who kept a closet full of stylish scarves, scented soaps, lint rollers, and razors; who owned and displayed a collection of complicated books. When I gave up on making a final determination, I became overrun with a new and anxious impatience. I just wanted to *see it* was all. But even this felt physical, like a panicked need for some drug, a craving for blood-red meat.

In brief, I wanted the creature to be something that would belong in a long winter coat and boots. I wanted him to quickly take the form of someone I would take for granted out of some age-old pattern of recognition: *This highly unremarkable human*, I would announce to whoever would listen, *is my dear son*. I'd imagine coming upon him on the street, in what was then his current state, an eyeless head fused to his chest, the suggestion of a tail still curling behind, and grew uneasy. No, better that he be a balding, middle-aged smoker of unfiltered cigarettes, his newness long ago dried all the way out. Better that he drank, was disappointed often, had a foul mouth. Better that I'd already fashioned for him the least remarkable of destinies than to be growing something I did not recognize at all. And better, too, that I be an old woman contented by the approach of her most ordinary creation than what I really was then, a fearful person full of unexamined thoughts about what is human and what is not, a nonpraying person pleading to no one in particular for her boy to be "right."

When spring came, I left the house to be outside, to marvel, at long last, at the beginning of a new season. In a new and much expanded form, I took to the sidewalks. Grass was greening up as daffodils suffused the air with halcyon calm, and strangers, I noticed, began smiling at me in passing, appearing to have gained a glimpse of the tiny new creature they'd already begun imagining in my arms. I had become something like a sign of spring, a spot of good news, a symbol of a not so terrible future to come. Stranger after stranger smiled, and it was as if somewhere along the way I'd picked up a basket full of kittens, the sheer gratuitousness of which was filling even the most cynical of souls with a rambling, exploratory hope. *Don't forget to have your pets spayed or neutered*, I said as I gave out the kittens one by one, abandoning myself to smiling into the smiling all around, one part of me pure, glittering Earth goddess, the other part a skeptic turned with bewilderment toward the public arrival of so much impulse, toward the bare broad side of every body's instinct for hope.

To fill the days, I also began chronicling the milestones not mentioned in the pregnancy books piled atop my nightstand. No one had yet written *Congratulations! At twenty-five weeks of gestation, your tiny baby's capacity for outsized resentment is already beginning to form!* But I drew it in myself, realizing that I'd already given rise to the exact moment when I'd be driving the car and he, the son, would be next to me, wearing his teenaged self like the world had nothing but room for it. I'd be driving, turning, and braking and otherwise thinning myself out on the logistics of taking good care, and he'd be quietly filling with disgust, thinking of my outdated hairstyle first, then my stained and pilled sweater, then the way I listened to public radio in the car like it was an act of virtue, one absolving me from the sin of living a life without any discernible impact at all—not on American foreign policy, not on election outcomes, not on genocides, inequality, or torture. But mostly he is annoyed with me for loving him even now, in this ungenerous moment, when he deserves it, he half suspects, the least. *Thanks for the ride,* he will say without meaning it, before getting out, growing up, not coming to realize (until a damp day in November of 2034) that I too had been capable of quietly wishing him gone. Was there any moment this body had not already begun? Any possibility left, as of yet, unborn? *There is not*, I called up with conviction from the airless burrow of my bed.

In the last to final days I took to groaning, in private, at home. I summoned food from where I lay. I wondered if the entire project would ever be done, if any of this would ever be named and normal, if our bodies would ever be made tidier by separation. And then one night in early summer, I completed the transformation, morphing momentarily into animal so that he could be born human and tiny and quivering, his mouth bleating out the disgruntled sound of a brand-new apprehension. He was stacked on top of me, chest to chest, where he kept low and held on tight. And when the nurse, who looked to me so clean and comfortable in her many cotton layers, told me it'd be easier next time, I could not decide if the words were for me, or what was the meaning of this casual *next time*.

So then the baby and I had become two bodies. Separate, we grew addicted to looking, to recognizing and being recognized, to keeping this loop going all day and all night. And then, being very busy with the looking and the diapering and the swaddling, it seemed only natural that I should also cease feeling nauseated with something like a sudden and unexplained lack of interest. I closed the front door on the varmint squirrels, the itinerant dogs, the ancient old women who continued to flank my house on all sides, they who delighted in turning my mind in farts and underarm smells, in the whiskers they held aloft on the same rotting breeze. In the end, I was weary. *Enough*, I said, *enough*, and then looked hard at my brutal little baby until it no longer seemed possible that he or any of the others had ever been inside. And so, just like that, I lost track of the mammoth we once made, but saved, for posterity, the memory of my body's great confusion, how for one lucid moment anything could've come of this.

My Youth

In 2003, when I was young and throwing myself for the first time onto America's churning, the Hummer, like a boulder on parade, rolled through the streets a symbol of U.S. power and might. The largest civilian vehicle ever manufactured and sold, the rumbling bulk of its body wanted people to know and admire its strength. *I am not*, it said without saying anything at all, *a Frenchman in tight black pants!* Indeed, the Hummer would never skirt around café tables with the litheness of a hungering cat or hold its cigarette too high like a woman. It was not human, did not dream of warm, washed skin, but it was no mere object either. In those days, it gathered my friends and me in the secondhand smoke of what we took to be the city's hippest bar and kept us there a good long while. In this pocket of carcinogens, we rounded up our scorn for it: the Hummer, which had made of guzzling a national virtue and a human right, which was, or so we'd heard, difficult to maneuver, stop, and store. And I think that maybe I can see now how things were then, me slim and spry and nodding, folding myself without consequence into the night never-ending, while the cold, clean air of a most certain war waited on nobody and on nothing outside.

These many years later, my youth and the cultural moment for deriding the Hummer have both wandered away gone. The Hummer out of production, other enormous SUVs an unremarkable feature of our streets, we have taken to demarking this America as hostile to that one using different instruments instead. Things have changed, time has passed, or some such sentence I am reluctant to write. In the present, I gesture to the everyday proof of my own time passing, the existence of my child, the occasional experience of temporal dissonance that comes with accruing age. These days I push my toddler son home from daycare in his stroller, passing by the empty parking lot of the VFW, and feel with the closing of my throat the meaning of our age difference and the urgency of determining what it is I need to tell him. *Let me tell you about my youth*, I start out, an old man turning without fanfare to topics of great importance, his recollections riding confident thrusts of bad breath. *When I was very young, inevitability was everywhere*, I say. *Our vehicles would only get bigger. Our soldiers would go to war.*

But what follows is necessarily a stammering.

In "The War at Home," a documentary about anti-war protests on the University of Wisconsin campus during America's war in Vietnam, a white male police officer beats a white male college student with his baton in a corner of Ingraham Hall that I, a student there some thirty years later, recognized only as the location of my favorite ATM. What I mean, perhaps, is that this war had been built on that one, that both are unending, that I was in my time and of my time but that I was also standing, with hand held out to clasp a brand new twenty, one world away from war's violence.

In March of 2003 I protested the American invasion of Iraq under a statue of Abraham Lincoln turning green from contact with old air and old time and we, the small but angry crowd of college students, sparked fear in the heart of no one. We didn't succeed in drawing masses up from library mall and onto Bascom Hill, and we didn't produce swells that dropped down to collect thousands of others. This war, as everyone knew then, was already going to happen. Student reporters covering the protest wrote then that folly was a rational human being resisting a war founded on facts, that this war would make the world a much safer place. And what I remember most about those days is that I spent them gasping, unable to believe how quickly and with what ease the story had already been written. But here I'm also at risk of suggesting, in that sly, self-interested way of memory, that in the year 2003 I was all these things: young, pretty, *right*.

What really lingers, I think, what needs to be said, is that time took care of the distinctions I thought I was making on that day and in the days that followed. I couldn't, or didn't, hold onto the facts forever. And time would take care of my need to yell too, the years slowly turning that red-hot pool of protest into a resigned and almost pleasurable sipping, the satisfaction of being informed in some highly informed place, the kind of coffee shop in the kind of neighborhood in the kind of city where we will all know the numbers—at least 200,000 Iraqi and Americans dead—but continue to measure our mornings in cupped silence, in clinks of spoon on saucer, in the privilege of sipping hot beverages over the terrible news of the day.

But I should start again.

The story begins when I leave the protest. When I cease being a campus protestor, when I cease worrying my parents, when I head to a parking lot where a young man, exotic with Waspyness, waits for me in the NPR of his black Honda Civic. I bounce into the passenger seat, my adrenaline still flowing from having yelled atop the puffed-up chest of my university, and I show him the homemade sign in my hand: "Send *Students* Abroad, Not Soldiers!" I cannot recall his response, but I know for a fact that I say to him next, as if confessing a pleasure, "I couldn't resist." And then I think we roll down the hill, past the view of the lake and toward the dim-lit warmth of some cheap bar or restaurant, all the while feeling electric and elated for having found one another in such interesting times, for having happened upon the soft youth of the other while we were both lingering at the exact same center of the universe.

Now, as the car rolls away, I see failure of imagination flowing from the tailpipe. I see how I thought I'd just been successful in going on record, how I thought I'd driven something immutable about myself into waiting ground. The war would happen, yes, but history would show that I'd been on the right side of it. And this identity—this having been *against*—would save me somehow, would absolve me of the complexity, the narrative, to come. When I wanted to stop the war, I thought I wanted the impossible. But what I could not see then was that it was my second-choice desire, the one I wanted fulfilled if the first could not be met that reeked of fantasy—that I would somehow be excised from the horror of my country's wars, that I would somehow be lifted free, by dint of my virtue and special feeling, of any obligation or responsibility, that I would have what no one could or should: a license to ignore the inhuman in me always.

Let me tell you, I say to a son who lives in soft new skin, who runs away from me often but who always comes back for more words, his mind sussing out the matters of the world. *This, a munching squirrel; that, a big oak tree. (We don't put that in our mouths; we don't stand on the table; we are gentle with our faces.)* There's so much to explain, but there's also the problem of knowledge falling apart, of stories losing arrangement over time.

After college and in the fall of 2003, I left the country to take a job teaching English to French schoolchildren in a small community in rural Normandy. There, on the second week of classes, one of the teachers pulled me aside to present me with a large stack of what in my own school days we called weekly readers, newspapers written especially for school children about the news of the day. He fanned them a bit, each of them containing a headline about America's war in Iraq, before dropping them in the arms of his *assistante*. "It might help you to read these," he said, "so you can see how we explain your war to the children." For the rest of a long, lonely year, the papers gathered dust and junk in the corner of my tiny one-room apartment, reminding me of the moment in which I'd received them. I'd lie on my foam mattress on the floor, eye level with that stack of papers, attempting to find reasonable words for my indignation, the perfect French for what could've been my most eloquent defense.

Thank you, Monsieur Vivien. I was against this war, I could've begun then, but didn't. *J'étais contre cette guerre, Monsieur Vivien*. But then the words would fail to come together in any honest way and I'd have to shift tactics and begin somewhere else, further back, with the story of my life, with history as I understood it, with more failures of speaking and thinking. Perhaps I'd said nothing because I didn't have anything to say, or because I couldn't, in that moment or any of the moments that followed, find a single fail-proof way in which the war wasn't mine. And poor Monsieur Vivien, who had not been told in advance who I was, who could not be expected to gather, not even from his years of watching American movies, that I was Jenny in *Forrest Gump* before all the drugs crept in, that while I was in his classroom leading the children in a chant of "One, two, buckle my shoe!" I was also charging, with Robin Wright's exquisite cheekbones, across the reflecting pool of the National Mall in a billowing white dress.

The story might also begin more recently, with me standing in an off-season curling club, its huge concrete floor now awash with used children's goods being sold on consignment. Here I'm whipping through a rack of clothing when I come upon a toddler T-shirt that all but drains the blood from my heart: still in its original tags, marked "organic cotton," the shirt's lone screen-printed image is that of a Hummer, the word "Bummer" appearing in large letters beneath. I hold the shirt in my hands, where at first I revile it for being a fifteen-year-old joke never once washed or worn, but where soon enough it begins pointing its uselessness at me and something very low thuds inside.

On this sales floor, I think I see how things really were then, or what it was we'd been making this whole time—the Hummer, T-shirts making fun of the Hummer, wars. In fact, the story of my youth, in its entirety, appears to have finally turned up here, in this used-up mountain of self-styled things, the tangled work of so many hands, a history from which no person or object is free. I try for the slip of one second to imagine pulling the Hummer shirt, emblem of my inevitable youth, down over the soft belly of my son. But what I find myself imagining instead is taking him captive, tying him to a chair with the thickening strap of my cautionary tales. About things that idle like life, or like death, but on and on and on. About my shame and its engine, about how even now, in a lucid state of regret, I stand ready to keep a comforting distance between myself and my power. About everything that goes missing each time a story begins.

Let me tell you about my youth, I might say, breezy this time, a middle-class mother pushing her son under flowering trees home from the good daycare she can pretty much afford. *I was the fourth child born to a milk hauler and a homemaker. I was raised among grandmas and grandpas, green hills and long valley views, wood chopping, sweet corn shucking,* Hee Haw, *Hot Wheels, and hot rods. I was born into dairy, the birth took twenty minutes, and then I went to college. I turned up to campus a knee-wobbling calf and there began licking salt from the desks and chairs and the floors, from the faces of weary professors, from the bindings on every single book. In fact, I filled a forgotten corner of the library's stacks with hay and slept there most nights, curling my youth into the wisdom of the world already written.*

A cow? the son ventures. But my knuckles whiten as I tighten the stroller's course. *People will tell you stories.*

Layers of Ice

In the mind's eye, Antarctica is more like the moon and less like Earth. But for all its whiteness—its galactic hints at nothingness—Antarctica comes laden with tales that, having risen out of nothing but ash and myth, stand like the continent's lone obelisks. For a place that cannot hold a footprint, the Antarctic bears well the markers of the travelers who've fallen upon it—people who've gone far for the sake of a good yarn or for the odorless smell of escape, people who've come to bellow and command dominion where few have bellowed and commanded before. Even before its discovery, when its existence was still just a rumor in the bloodshot eye of the sea captain, a question mark on globes of the day, a *Terra Australis Incognita,* Antarctica was a wellspring of mystery and fabrication, a kind of dreamscape meant for philosophers and fantasists and not just for the measuring tools of men. This is how, after a daring and inaugural submarine voyage in Antarctic seas, Jules Verne's Captain

Nemo came to grace the pole in 1868, sticking it with a flag marked "N." Or how, in 1818, an American named John Cleves Symmes Jr. could theorize that exploration of the poles would eventually reveal 1,400-mile-wide holes dropping down into the void of the Earth. This is speculation rich in imagery, and like many things Antarctic, it smacks of hearsay made permanent somehow.

Antarctica's vast record of nonfictional heroes is no less captivating. Even those who lost their lives on the continent or on its shores still live on to speak highly of the place. Nowadays, red-cloaked personnel from the nearby American base, Ross Island's McMurdo Station, can crack open the door to Scott's Hut still standing on Cape Evans—headquarters for his fatal trek to the pole in 1911—and peruse the preserved innards of the expedition's quotidian: beakers, notebooks, a London newspaper, stacked and sunken wooly bunks, and, in the galley corner, fourteen mugs hanging on hooks, full bottles of ketchup, canned haddock, pea flour, smoked veal, and crates of hot cocoa, all of it left untouched by the desert climate. Scott's hut endures, but more than that, it stands ready. Its wooden door opens and offers up the Heroic Age's hormones, lays the dust and must of reality all around, and—closing itself against the wind outside—invites admiration for the thrills of men who, though long dead, seem always to be up to something, men who must rise up in ghostly visions of sinew and forearm, of unshaven faces and brooms brushing the floor, to do their legacy's housekeeping when no one else is around.

Always separate, always unapologetic, Antarctica also seems the lone continent with an ongoing license to occupy mythical spaces in addition to real ones. This is, of course, a place of facts and expensive science: ice core samples that read like the new history book, alarming data on Earth's warming, neutrino hunting, NASA equipment seemingly worth more than its weight in gold, and geological dust samples bagged and labeled for future scientific study and publication. But it's also rich in those man-made myths, the messy and inexplicable record of human travel and sweat, some of that reaching and all that failing. Our mythical Antarctica, if solidly anything at all, is the strange logic of willed hardship, the dubious rewards of conquest, and the ballast-like dignity of a life lived in pursuit of knowing and dreaming the unknown. Antarctica, when real, imagined, or drifting somewhere in between, proves that we are still captive to the mystery in distance, still loyal to the pledge found in story.

—

I arrived on board a C-17, a military plane so large, gray, and windowless that it reduces mileage to an abstraction. The distance, and the fact that we were at that moment covering it, seemed like something occurring far outside the borders of that vast and intriguing in-air country, where roughly a hundred people of all ages and sizes sat sweating in all the same gear, eating the same sack lunches, similar hints of pluck and boredom in their upward turned eyes. And so when the plane stopped moving forward on a surface I could not yet see but which was, presumably, on or near the bottom of the world, I stood up to search the faces of those around me.

The door opened, a collective cheer went up, and cold gusted in. I didn't yet know my fellow laborers well and so the moment still seemed my own rite of passage, the ego-filled gift sometimes offered to the solitary explorer. I pulled on some more clothes I'd been issued in New Zealand, took up another couple bags of extreme cold weather gear, and stood to wait for the line forming in the aisle to advance. I studied the touchable whiteness pouring in from the hatch and transferred my weight to my toes, leaning toward and into my long-awaited moment of lucidity. Descending the stairs with the same bewildered grin I saw on several faces around me, I at once assessed the cold, the ice, and the light. In that first moment of foreignness, McMurdo dutifully played the shocking part of small outpost at the end of the world. Its steam rose in the distance, signs of life and industry emitting from a tiny town otherwise clinging in isolation to an outcrop of faraway earth. I watched the bungled efforts of my enormous white boots crossing the ice shelf in adolescent thuds and settled into the feeling of flight. Right then, while peering down, I began claiming my own small sites of discovery.

—

McMurdo welcomed with daylit night, with single digit spring temperatures, a wind chill factor well below zero, and the confused onslaught of a strange sampling of details: the look of white snow that had drifted in and against crumbled black rock; the gloomy architecture of station, its ground-running pipes and partitions functioning like industrial-sized mousetraps; distant mountain ranges that mystified my Midwestern eye; the dark personal space allotted me in the dorm room I shared with three others, my own stacked and quartered bunk section existing in semi-privacy just inches below the ceiling; and, finally, the reassuring abundance of salad greens served up in the galley that evening. Too new to realize these greens had come in as cargo on the same flight I had, I also didn't know that, on station, these were known as "freshies." Called so in covetous tones, freshies were for scavenging, not always available, more than anything else only there until gone. Unwittingly, I walked into station ritual, lifted lettuce up onto my plate.

"Mac-Town," as it is called by those fluent in the language of the Ice, was assembled in 1956 by the U.S. Navy from what must have been a large import of pipes, steel beams, and metal siding. Its naval roots give it the sharply utilitarian look of a hardy but graying military base and expose the station's original, somehow tacit genesis: an Antarctic foil to communism that these days seems both improbable and abstract. A year after its construction, when the first International Geophysical Year was celebrated, it also became the center of U.S. scientific operations in Antarctica, a role it has played ever since.

McMurdo stands on Ross Island and therefore at the center of landmarks serving as points of reference for the earliest expeditions: Observation Hill, an enormous and steeply graded mound rising out of the backside of town; Discovery Hut, the bleakest and coldest of British explorer Robert F. Scott's shelters (unwisely modeled after houses built in the Australian outback); nearby Castle Rock, an ominous and rugged edifice sitting atop an area hiding deadly crevasses; and, forty miles off, Mount Erebus, which emits a delicate plumage of still gaseous activity while simultaneously existing as almost everyone's secret darling. At the center of all these markers sits the station, with its culture of numbers, nicknames, and abbreviations. Naming both the landscape and buildings—all those points placed on the psychic map—becomes part of coming to know this place, speaking its language, acquiescing in the face of its rough and charming efforts at seduction. To live on station, I learned quickly, means to roll oneself right into its looping tendency toward the self-referential, to never look at it alone.

—

On the Ice, just as on Earth, all jobs are not created equal. Contrary to what some people seemed to believe when I informed them I was going to Antarctica, work is scarce at the bottom of the world. In fact, even the mere possibility of gaining employment on the Ice forms long lines of able-bodied people waiting to be called up, medical paperwork crinkled in outstretched hands. The only reason I'd gotten a job at all was because I'd shown my readiness, as well as the naiveté necessary, to take the worst one the place could muster. As a DA (dining attendant), working for the corporate subcontractor responsible for all the station's laborers, or nonscientific personnel, I debarked the plane only to be at work the next morning by six. The next day I scrubbed all that the galley had to offer and began doing so nine hours a day, six days a week, in obvious ignorance of the outside world.

Not involved in food preparation, the DA job is essentially to keep all serving areas, serving tools, and pots and dishes spotless—a task better saved for Sisyphus, as it goes on in an endlessly cyclical way, beginning or finishing again with each of the four meals served daily to the summer population of roughly 1,000. My workday was divided up into perfectly timed—it is not melodramatic to say robotic—increments of dishwashing, pot scrubbing, mopping, vacuuming, emptying, and refilling interspersed with short, unofficial moments of groaning as well as exchanging lifesaving snippets of sardonic wit with the other dozen DAs standing by in the DA uniform: black elastic-band pants, blue polo, black no-slip shoes, baseball cap, and a trickle of liquid excrement from the food waste bins spreading like a sad badge of honor across the chest.

As a DA, one works on Sunday when the rest of the station has the day off. And one works on holidays too, serving up special meals as the rest of the community sits down together for the feast. As a DA—the position with the worst safety rate on station due to the high risk of repetitive motion injuries—you are told how to spray, how to lift, how to scrub, how to turn, how to stand, even how to sleep. "Your fingers outstretched all the way, your palms flat," we were told one day by the station's physical therapist, "in a praying position." This directive also happened to mirror my own thoughts each night as I lay in bed compulsively stretching the tight tendons of my fingers and forearms and fretting about carpal tunnel.

Every morning I'd wake up to the task of parting with my body. To do the job as I was told to do it (told, that is, repeatedly, pedantically, and with top-down allusions to my season-end bonus) was to reconcile myself to the fact that my body was no longer mine. In a twist both ironic and predictable, my anger at management or the mechanization of my life would sometimes get channeled into hard work. Back in the damp and balmy netherworld of the pot room, cathartic screams of metal lyrics such as "God told me to skin you" helped me scrub pots all the faster and also put the finishing touches on the age-inappropriate teenage rebellion I'd been experiencing as of late—a rebellion stinking, as it always does, of injustice, or the desire to slight as you've been slighted, to fling the poo back.

To really know the DA, however, is to see her elsewhere, after hours and out of uniform but still smelling of food scraped three times from the same dish. Entering either of the two bars on station any night of the week one is bound to encounter both of these groups: the horny and underutilized firefighters, men just this side of pubescence who are paid well for their opportunity to be drunk on ice; and the wisecracking dining attendants who, having first arrived with a shared love for great music or great literature, now must gather to drink, bash, and purge, who safeguard their growing sense of mutiny with a group therapy that calls only for a circle of withering, a culture of spit, who explore the darkest reaches of their resentment, and then do their best to walk it home.

—

Red was broad shouldered, big, late twenties, with hair as brisk namesake, and a large, almost electrified presence. He hovered over me in the hallway of 155—the building in which I slept and worked—and played the veteran to my rookie, sage to my shrinking presence. He was looking in on me because he too was from Wisconsin, because he went to college with my second cousin, and because a coworker of mine had put us in contact before I went down to Antarctica. His last stateside email to me had finished with what I read as wistful flourish: "I guess you could say the Ice has been good to me."

Having worked every summer season since college at McMurdo, as well as one long and dark winter, Red was a regular of the Ice. He was a local figure of sorts, and this in Antarctica, where no one is local, where becoming indigenous means coming to work here repeatedly, successively, every season for years, usually with your own quirky offering to the community forming and re-forming there. Some, for example, go with a fair amount of eccentricity in tow, or a secret artist's life, others a bullheaded bachelor credo stinking of ex-wives, or a love of living and drinking in cold weather climates. The "lifers" earn wrinkled faces marked by years of cold wind and continuous sun and walk around in eerie and unexamined union with the place. Red, for his part, brought boisterousness, a love of people, and a willingness to run an informal cash bar out of his dorm room. He also had some wisdom to impart. "Are you liking it?" he asked with congenial forcefulness.

I looked down. My feet hurt. I was tired and hadn't had a complete thought in weeks. I'd barely been outside. I felt small in his presence and wished I could meet him with a little energy in my face, a little optimism in the shoulders.

"I am glad I came," I answered, and he eyed me with suspicion.

"You're 'one and done,' huh?" He said, referring to the number of seasons I planned to work on the Ice.

I shrugged: Who knows? Yeah. Maybe.

"You're not one of these people who comes for one season so that they can write a book about it, are you?" There was legitimate leeriness in his voice. I wrapped myself in a "no," a protective gesture, remembering little of the writer buried deep in the stink of the DA uniform, and Red went back to laughing and cajoling. Red gave me more advice of the "Just love it, kid" variety and then, washing his hands of me, turned to walk down the hallway in search of more shoptalk, more antics. I turned away too. But for me it was to go climb into that bunk just below the ceiling, to take the weight off my feet, to lazily scrawl some variation of "Pots, Dishes, Pots" onto the thick stack of my journal's blank and expectant pages. I drained the blood off a workday by falling asleep.

—

While working in the galley, the larger landscape of station remained unexplored. McMurdo was a small, industrial conglomeration of unknown buildings with unknown functions; I wasn't sure how much of anything worked, where the water was kept, or the fuel, or the wood shop, or the power plant, or where it was that the scientists went. My knowledge of the Ice was limited to moments of recreation taking place on my day off, half of which I usually spent sleeping. I knew a couple of hiking trails, Gallagher's (the nonsmoking bar), the two nonautomated bowling lanes, the Gerbil Gym, and the Coffee House. Letters and emails from home, in the meantime, were all versions of a question that hungered for story. "Antarctica?" they asked.

I memorized McMurdo's people from what felt like my omnipresence on the galley floor. Behind the baseball cap I wore low, I observed the station's residents and noticed who was sloppy, who was considerate, who was quick to scoop up the potatoes, who always took dessert. I even annoyed a man once by telling him beforehand what it was he was about to select from the buffet. And sometimes I'd watch for the old man rumored to have taken a snowmobile all the way up the side of Erebus decades ago (when, the regulars assured us, there had been fewer rules on the Ice, when things *really* used to get wild around here). When he came by for lunch or dinner, I'd snap at the hot pink kitchen gloves worn to protect me from buffet burns, follow his quick step with my eyes, and analyze his eating habits or think on the aging dent of his spine.

Werner Herzog, the filmmaker, was also there. Having come as a part of the Antarctic Artists and Writers Program to film a documentary backed by Discovery Films, he walked around like one of us, albeit a more famous and possibly more possessed version—one that was often trailed by an equally Germanic looking cinematographer sometimes seen running the camera. Herzog was tall, in his sixties, always polite in the galley, with a face that looked incapable of fatigue, and instinctually—or as a force of habit perhaps—*interested*. He was full of close looks and quick bursts of faraway-seeming observation. He had a way of taking in the whole galley, his eyebrows ticking off notes, before sitting down to eat. The rumor, substantiated in the station's weekly newspaper, which ran several articles on Herzog while he was there, was that he was working on the unorthodox Antarctic documentary. At the time, he was threatening a total absence of penguins. That was not, he said, what interested him about the Ice. What did interest him occurred quickly to this station of eccentrics. Known for his mythmaking, his hero worship, his knack for finding and drawing out people with bizarre or impossible goals, an unfiltered sense of possibility, quirky lifestyles, Herzog was not merely tolerated, he was welcomed, cooperated with even, as if the collective message delivered to him each morning over breakfast was "You've found your material in us."

—

One Saturday night, sixty-some people crowded into Gallagher's, the small and windowless bar, for the Freak Train, a variety show organized by recreation personnel. A colorful succession of idiosyncratic moments took the stage one after the other, a typically McMurdoesque cornucopia of wigs, leisure suits, tutus, tattoos, and empty cans of Speight's. And as the show plodded on in strange and funny increments, so did the efforts of Herzog and his cinematographer, both of whom leaned in to within feet of the performers' beads of sweat to capture everything: the sexy young belly dancer donning a fake beard; the tiny middle-aged woman folding herself into an orange extreme cold weather gear bag (her boyfriend then picking her up); the quirky, hipster take on traditional church spirituals; a Colonel Sanders look-alike making grasshopper noises; and songwriters singing accolades for McMurdo's heavy equipment, doing so in the kind of Ice language that speaks wryly and exclusively of the one-station universe.

Standing in the back and sipping at my cheap glass of wine, I laughed often. The Freak Train's every antic was filmed and the bar's adrenaline was palpable, just one more existent oddity for that room, that place. But I also soon became fascinated by Herzog's forehead, lined as it was in both sweat and anticipation, and I wondered then about the naked fervor in this whole performance. Who was watching what here, and what was being performed for whom?

And of course I couldn't help but notice the way the camera kept catching me standing there in the back. I was imagining the gaze of far distant television viewers and saw myself as seen from the other end of that portal: that brunette sweating and drinking in the musk of community, in the hot and unlikely confines of a bar all the way at the bottom. How many of us, I wondered as I studied Herzog and this room full of bodies, were dragging our lives off the map just to get it on record? How many of us were voyeurs gone adventuring?

—

Nearly ten months prior, I'd applied online for jobs at McMurdo on something like existential whim. Young and not feeling that I was otherwise up to much, one day I'd fallen into an afternoon of direct sunlight and recumbent dreaming. How, I wondered idly, does one begin scripting one's life? I roused myself into a sitting position and turned to the navigational practices of my day. I googled "Working in Antarctica." Months later, while stuffing envelopes at my stable but sedate job, I was surprised to receive a phone call from Polar Services, but had the good sense to take my phone, my adrenaline, and my bones' subdued jangling into the supply closet to set up an interview for the following week. In my phone interview I heard myself assuring someone—a gruffly voiced woman—that, in addition to being capable of lifting fifty pounds with ease, I was also what I deemed "psychologically fit." Even then there was a total absence of fear or sense of consequence, as if shameless self-promotion were the key to weightlessness here on Earth. Indeed, on the phone I was flawless, larger than life, an eloquent kind of burly. And yet it was not long after I hung up that I began running and lifting weights. Worried that a Polar omniscient might one day find me out and shred my file for being all waif and bone, all mouth and no meat, I got up to do the training I dreamed would finally make good on those fifty pounds.

The Worst Journey in the World, the nearly 600-page tome by Apsley Cherry-Garrard, probably holds one of the most vaunted places in the library of adventure narratives. The youngest man along, Cherry was only twenty-four when he joined Scott on his last expedition, which lasted from 1910 to 1913. Eventually, this adventure left him waiting at Cape Evans while the realization that Scott's polar party was never coming back crept slowly down the hut walls. Written when middle-aged and still haunted by the early and tragic summit of his life's experience, by ailments and illness he would long associate with that expedition, in the last paragraph Cherry nevertheless leans in to urge his readers to do as he has done: "And I tell you, if you have the desire for knowledge and the power to give it a physical expression, go out and explore."

I am going, I used to tell people, *because I can,* and some days this seemed like explanation enough.

—

When Herzog invited the community to screen his 2004 documentary *The White Diamond*, many of us jumped at the chance, filing into the galley's dining area to watch the movie on a large screen on the wall and skirting far away from Frosty Boy—the silver beast always humming and clunking away at our soft serve—before choosing a seat. The shades drawn against the omnipresence of the sun, we nestled into the novelty of watching art with the artist, asking Herzog himself our questions, and hearing the philosophy of one man's work come out in an English tangled with Germanic chomps.

The film featured one man's dream of a certain kind of aviation—a helium-filled balloon and flying machine designed to explore forest canopies—and did so with purely arresting footage of the Guyana rainforest, of that man's unbridled intensity, of a local waterfall crisscrossed by the flight patterns of swifts. I succumbed almost immediately to the whispered quality of all this dreaming even as the film got sticky with interpersonal conflict or turned tangential and therefore even stranger with footage of a local Rastafarian, Marc Antony, who slowly and earnestly narrates the beauty all around him or expounds upon his love for a rooster. Knowledgeable about the rainforest as source of natural medicine, Marc Antony is also followed into the dewy forest where he holds up a twig of something curing arthritis pain. Later on, when he emerges onto a precipice overlooking the waterfall, the camera focuses on a drop of water falling from a leaf and Herzog calls out to him, "Marc Antony, do you see a whole universe in this one single drop of water?"

At this, Marc Antony turns to the camera with a moon-touched smirk. "I cannot hear what you say for the thunder that you are," he replies almost inaudibly.

In Herzog's post-film talk, he lightly, casually, mentioned that this moment had been scripted. Seeming amused by the question he asks Marc Antony in that scene, he brushed it off as a "stupid, New Age question." To a room now very silent, he also mentioned that the film made use of bird calls not indigenous to Guyana. Of course, Herzog said, some bird lover somewhere can always catch him on that stuff, can be one of the three hundred people in the world who can recognize that note as false.

I listened as Herzog continued to explain his choices, drawing the distinction between what he called the factual truth and the ecstatic truth, or "the ecstasy of truth." I had so loved the sweeping scenes of waterfall and bird, the chirping sound of that impossible-seeming choir, and did not know what to make of this new reality, this layer of myth now worked in long ago, unable to be extracted from my story. I also thought suddenly of the galley's salad boy, a very young man suspected of being a pathological liar but to whom Herzog and his camera seemed to be drawn from the start.

Not alone, I could sense the questions of others in attendance. The room now seemed split between those who felt admiration for Herzog's art, his genius, his long history of mythmaking, his ability to cast spells, and those who were troubled by what he'd presented as technicality, but which could be seen as a deviation from the truth, a bit of deception hiding in his depiction. A young, earnestly bearded man stood to ask a question. He had the look of someone who, in the off-season, negotiated the realities of a cabin life in Alaska—where fish and firewood exist as material, nonnegotiable truths. "Doesn't," he asked, "the inclusion of those fabrications detract from the real story? Why bother to include them at all?"

At least half the room—people who work in Antarctica, many of whom I saw as having a rich sense of story—seemed to nod in agreement. I imagined these people returning home with only responsible representations of life on the Ice, people who, weary of the world's appetite for story, would simply scold the ignorant people they met in bars, "There *are* no polar bears in Antarctica," and then turn away, accurate, but alone.

—

Halfway through my four-month season, I had a stroke of good and unimaginable luck. Through a discreet grapevine of nongalley folks, I was contacted about interviewing for another job on station. The shuttles office, the department responsible for transporting scientists and all other personnel from station to the ice-shelf's airfield twenty-four hours a day, seven days per week, needed one more. This was the kind of chance we, in the galley, were told never to expect, so I went about interviewing for it quietly and with only a surreal sense at best of the possibility for escape.

After interviewing and being cleared for the new position by the shuttles office, I went to see the executive chef, a tiny woman reviled by DAs, with my detached heart in hand. She made it clear that it was she who controlled my fate, annunciating the word *contract* for me more than once as I sat in her office wondering how I'd ended up here, my fate in the hands of someone wound tight into the strange shape of her ergonomic chair. She implied that I should think long and hard about what leaving the galley family would mean but also eventually indicated that she was willing to let me go. I was not, like most family members I can think of, irreplaceable, and so they'd just bring another someone down to the Ice to take my place. She took time to impress upon me how rare my transfer was. "This is like winning the lottery," she scolded as we scheduled my last day of work. I knew enough to say little. I began counting down the silent days.

—

When I arrived to the ice shelf of the Ross Sea for the second time it was at the wheel of Ivan the Terrabus, a poppy-red monster boasting all-wheel drive, three axles, balloon tires that came to my chin, and a $600,000 price tag. Where once

I could not be trusted to move my fingers and limbs without direction, I was now in command of a vehicle with a turning range like that of a freightliner, one capable of transporting up to fifty-five souls. Sadly, many of my galley suspicions were immediately confirmed. Everyone else really was making an easier living on the Ice. Some people really were required to do almost nothing at all. And, finally, left alone in a vehicle roaring along groomed snow roads, the icy white Antarctic finally became the source of a real and everyday enchantment. I routinely greeted Mount Erebus on my left. My eyes ran with whimsy along the Royal Society mountain range thirty miles to my right. I wondered about the exact direction of the pole, or watched clouds appear out of nowhere, moving above me on some other mysterious expanse.

Not without a considerable amount of survivor's guilt, I also kneeled down to gather up my autonomy again, to pick up the tiny beads of my life gone spilled on the ground. I reveled in wearing my jeans to work. I spent the dead time in between runs reading, sometimes one book for every twelve-hour shift, and wrote copiously in a journal. Alone in the large van that had to stand ready to taxi at the runway, I would watch fog roll in and around me in what felt like seconds, exhaling long and grandiose thoughts about vastness, about outer space, about Antarctica, about the necessity of our heavily flagged routes, about all things seeming larger and truer than life.

Did I find my ice and myth? Wearing my Carhartts, my yellow leather driving gloves, or pushing my matted hair back into my stocking cap as I shifted or turned astride Ivan,

I drove in partial costume, with an eye turned toward the camera. "Antarctica?" the letters still read, but now I had an answer: this big bus, that wind, my work boots, those mountains. Troubled by the ease with which I could now answer, I knew that I'd found my adventure in more than one form, that I had seen what it wasn't before seeing what it was, that I carried in my chest the myth and the anti-myth, and that they coalesced uneasily there. I grew haunted by my responsibility to tell it all right—from grease-caked pans to spying on the universe from the portal of my windowed cab. Because it had a way of telling a story all on its own, speaking of history, hugeness, and dominion, and putting me automatically behind the wheel, I grew reluctant to share my Ivan image. What does one do, after all, with an image that can't be explained, the image whose truth is obscured by myth, and whose myth gets sapped by a search for accuracy? I could explain it as Herzog might—with script, with the ecstasy of truth, with a license to craft my own story. In the end, I could disentangle myself from the constraints of everyday Earth.

—

One very dull day, the ubiquitous mythmaker comes upon her as she is just barely managing to hoist a large gas nozzle up and over her head. [This is the absurd and solitary moment of a small woman refueling her mammoth bus.] *On this slow day, he seems to find her interesting enough, leans in to disturb her with a forehead hot and humming, and asks some questions in an odd and foreign cadence.*

Does driving Ivan make you feel like a celestial being?

Does the universe whisper to you on all this wind?

Do you dream of driving this bus all the way back to Wisconsin?

Her answers surface unsaid one by one. They are fast and inspired. They rise from the bottom, out of nothing, to exist in half forms, in woolly permanence. But to Herzog, that wealthy collector, she gives silence. In the end, she turns to the camera and smiles at those who will recognize this note as false. [The camera stays on her a long, long time.]

—

There is deep possibility in the blindness of a place belonging to no one. Here, there are myths to be scrapped and then replaced with your own. Here, even the wind backs your anecdotic endeavor, originating as it does in places too far away to give any good reasons for why not. Off the map with no compass I did my fair share of the shrug and wander, but I also came to live in camaraderie with those who came before, those who had once done it bigger, had described it all so much better, those who knew a bit about the problem of telling. When February came and my name appeared on the list for redeployment, I crossed the ice shelf to reboard the plane with a crystal pillaged from Erebus sitting like a story in my pocket. *Homeward*, I thought, *is the journey burdened by bright new lies.*

Notes

Insider's Almanac

For this essay, I consulted several books on Aldo Leopold and his remarkable legacy, most notably two books by Curt D. Meine: *Aldo Leopold: His Life and Work* (Madison: University of Wisconsin Press, 1988) and *Correction Lines: Essays on Land, Leopold, and Conservation* (Washington, DC: Island Press, 2004), as well as *The Essential Aldo Leopold: Quotations and Commentaries* edited by Curt D. Meine and Richard L. Knight (Madison: University of Wisconsin Press, 1999). I also found Ursula Heise's *Sense of Place and Sense of Planet: The Environmental Imagination of the Global* (New York: Oxford University Press, 2008) useful in thinking through this essay.

The Painted Forest

In addition to the fraternalism scholarship mentioned in this essay, I also consulted *Secret Ritual and Manhood in Victorian America* by Mark C. Carnes (New Haven: Yale University Press, 1991) and *Morals and Markets: The Development of Life Insurance in the United States* by Viviana A. Rotman Zelizer (New York: Columbia University Press, 1979). I'm also fully indebted to Lisa Stone and Leslie Umberger, whose research into the life and paintings of Ernest Hüpeden was critical to writing this essay. Works consulted include *Sacred Spaces and Other Places: A Guide to Grottos and Sculptural Environments in the Upper Midwest* by Lisa Stone (Chicago: School of the Art Institute of Chicago Press, 1993); *Sublime Spaces and Visionary Worlds: Built Environments of Vernacular Artists* by Leslie Umberger, with contributions by Erika Doss, Ruth DeYoung Kohler, Lisa Stone, and Jane Bianco (New York: Princeton Architectural Press, 2007); and "Ernest Hüpeden: Beyond the Forest" written by Lisa Stone and Leslie Umberger and published by Edgewood College in conjunction with its August 2012 exhibit of Hüpeden's work. The essay's descriptions of DeMoulin's fraternal goats come from *Catalog No. 439: Burlesque Paraphernalia and Side Degree Specialties and Costumes* by Gary Groth and Charles Schneider (Seattle: Fantagraphics Books, 2010).

Acknowledgments

I'm deeply grateful to Derek Krissoff and the entire staff of the West Virginia University Press, as well as the In Place series editors, Elena Passarello and Jeremy B. Jones, for believing in this book and so carefully giving it life. For the book's title, I must thank Dolores Nash, who in the 1960s not only saved Woodman Hall from being repurposed as a garage but also poetically rechristened it the Painted Forest. For the time and space to get something done, I'm indebted to The Pennsylvania State University, the Virginia Center for Creative Arts, Isle Royale National Park's Artist-in-Residence program, the Crosshatch Center for Art and Ecology, Shake Rag Alley Center for the Arts, and former and current directors of the Painted Forest, David Smith and David Wells, both of Edgewood College. For buoying this work in a variety of ways, I thank the editors who first published many of these essays, as well as the Wormfarm Institute, the Council for Wisconsin Writers, and the Arts + Literature Laboratory. In Madison, I benefit from the company and counsel of talented writers and generous friends, including Angela Woodward, Sara Greenslit, Chris Mohar, Meghan O'Gieblyn, and Barrett Swanson. For my sanity, I am fully indebted to Morris Collins, a writer whose wisdom and friendship have made a great many things possible these past ten years. I also remain grateful to the character and the Captain himself, my good friend Chris Soma. This being a first book, I've got some early influences to acknowledge as well, including the Reedsburg Public Library, the Wuest family, and my writing teachers Dwight Worman, Rob Nixon, and Brian Lennon. For their steady support, I thank all my family and friends. For being the guardian of my solitude, I reserve my deepest thanks for my partner, D. Leith Nye. For being a human cannonball, which is to say for being exactly who he is, I also thank my dear son, Glen.